W9-BXD-435

Suicide and Euthanasia

Suicide and Euthanasia

THE RIGHTS OF PERSONHOOD

EDITED BY

Samuel E. Wallace

AND

Albin Eser

THE UNIVERSITY
OF TENNESSEE PRESS
KNOXVILLE

Manufactured in the United States of America.
First edition.

*Clothbound editions
of University of Tennessee Press books
are printed on paper designed for an effective life
of at least 300 years, and binding materials are chosen
for strength and durability.*

Library of Congress Cataloging in Publication Data

Main entry under title:

Suicide and euthanasia.

Bibliography: p.
Includes index.
1. Suicide—Addresses, essays, lectures.
2. Euthanasia—Addresses, essays, lectures.
3. Right to die—Addresses, essays, lectures.
I. Wallace, Samuel E. II. Eser, Albin. [DNLM:
1. Suicide. 2. Euthanasia. W864 S948]
HV6545.S82 179'.7 80-28799

to Mary Estena Talley Wallace

Acknowledgments

to Norman O. Brown, whose book *Life Against Death* significantly influenced my own thinking about death;

to Ernst Becker, whose *The Denial of Death* built on the masterful work of Brown while opening yet new avenues of thought;

to the widows who participated in my first research project on grief and bereavement, *After Suicide*, and who taught me the pain that suicide can cause;

to Lee Humphreys and Charles Jackson, who have taught death-related courses with me at the University of Tennessee and who have taught me much in other ways;

to Albin Eser, whose courageous 1975 West German Conference on Suicide and Euthanasia sparked my interest in the relationship between these two topics;

to the members of my own Wallace clan, especially my siblings, Bill, Mary Lea, Jean and Jane, Lucy, Don, and Lois, for whom I am but spokesman, as we have faced and shall continue to face death with dignity;

to my daughter, Michele, for carrying on Wallace traditions while enriching them, especially in our own house;

and to my partner in life and death, Susan.

—Samuel E. Wallace

Contents

Suicide and Euthanasia

Ω

Introduction

What does jumping off a bridge have to do with the mercy killing of a person presumed dying with an irreversible disease? How can the despair and irrationality associated with suicide be linked to the compassionate concern expressed by those who would commit euthanasia to end suffering? What, if any, is the relationship between suicide and euthanasia?

This volume is devoted to examining the relationship between suicide and euthanasia. Although previous publications have examined the relationship between suicide and other forms of death like homicide (Henry and Short, 1954), there are few books that systematically examine suicide and euthanasia. There is one series of papers published in German (Eser, 1976b) from a conference organized by Albin Eser, and indeed that conference was the starting point for this volume. Several separate articles have also mentioned some of the interrelationships between suicide and euthanasia (Rakoff, 1973; Kohl, 1974). Despite the foregoing suggestive leads, the relationship between suicide and euthanasia has yet to be explored.

In other comparisons between types of death, between suicide and homicide, for example, much about the nature of both types was learned. Because suicide and homicide were found to vary inversely, one increasing as the other decreased, societal pressures on individuals were seen to be either inwardly or outwardly directed: suicide was seen as violence directed toward self while homicide was perceived as violence directed toward the other. Further, comparative studies of suicide and homicide revealed that both involve considerations of the sanctity and quality of life. Some people may commit suicide rather than betray their religious beliefs, while others may commit homicide rather than allow those who have dishonored them or their loved ones to live.

The debate concerning suicide and euthanasia can also profit from considering them jointly because in part, as Fletcher flatly states in Chapter 3, "to justify either one, suicide or mercy killing, is to justify the other." Is life a universal good? Is it to be protected under all circumstances, even against suicide? What about cases of self-defense? If exceptions are to be allowed, how should the sanctity of life be weighed against the quality of life? What rights, if any, should individuals have over their own lives? over the lives of others? Regardless of the answers given to such questions, the debate about them reveals the interrelatedness of the quality of life and its sanctity.

The present volume also seeks to help fill a gap in the available literature. Publications in the area of death and dying have grown from a few scattered articles prior to the 1960s to considerable magnitude today. Whereas Freud (1933) wrote his early thoughts on the subject as part of a more general examination of the human psyche, and Lindeman (1944) published his early empirical study in a general journal of social psychology, scholars today have specialized journals devoted in whole or part to death and dying. In addition, other publications periodically devote entire issues to the specialized topics of death and dying (Lofland, 1976). Yet in spite of this increase in studies of death and dying, suicide and euthanasia remain relatively unexplored in terms of their relationship to each other.

Realizing this gap in the developing literature, Albin Eser organized a conference on suicide and euthanasia at the University of Bielefeld, Germany, in 1975. As an invited participant, Wallace, who had done research on suicide (1973), began to see euthanasia in a new light. Wallace and Eser agreed to work together after the conference on the related issues of suicide and euthanasia. The present volume represents the outcome of our collaboration.

Rather than simply present a series of papers with only an introductory comment, the editors have endeavored to use each article to trace the relationship between suicide and euthanasia. Further, an attempt has been made to develop a general perspective for examining both kinds of acts. We term our perspective "The Rights of Personhood."

The papers for this volume were chosen in part in order to raise the basic issues that are involved. The reader is also encouraged to enter the debate. The issues are complex and their resolution is of profound consequence. Later we shall refer to one authority who insists that after everything is considered the present system is the best. Perhaps. Before reaching that position, however, we all have the responsibility of considering the issues fully. If, after such consideration we opt for no change, we will do so fully aware of the consequences of our decision. Not to consider, not to discuss, disagree, and argue—that would be the far greater harm.

Ω

Death Is Social

Recent advances in medical technology have made it possible to sustain the bodily functions of a human being almost indefinitely. With the aid of machines, the heart can continue to pump blood, the lungs can continue to expand and to contract, and waste can be periodically evacuated. The question remains: is such a human being alive?

To answer that question the Harvard Medical School (1968) appointed a committee to define death. Because of recent technological developments, experts found that current definitions of death such as heart or respiratory stoppage were no longer sufficient. A new definition was needed to establish the point at which death can be considered to have occurred.

In its report the Harvard committee recommended that death be defined on the basis of brain waves. A flat electroencephalogram, indicating a lack of brain waves, is, they said, evidence that a human being could no longer sustain life if separated from mechanical support systems. Therefore, when test results yield a flat EEG, such humans should be considered to be without life.

In arriving at their new definition, the authorities challenged the popular view that death is a single event that happens in a single moment—"he died"; "she passed away." More extensive research revealed the process of dying, a series of stages involving different kinds of deaths: among them, organ death, brain death, and cellular death. At the present state of our technology, the process of dying is irreversible when brain death occurs, and so authorities today suggest the use of brain death as our best definition of the state of "being dead." In the future, when we may be able to reconstitute a human life from any one of its cells (by cloning), today's definition of death as brain death will probably be as obsolete as the definition of death as respiratory failure is now. Perhaps no less than cellular death may later suffice as a definition. The essential point is that, however defined, death consists of stages, of one type of death at this point and then another kind at another point. Dying is a process involving a series of "deaths" that today become irreversible only when brain death is reached.

All of the stages included thus far in the process of dying are confined to the neurophysiological level. The literature on death and dying is dominated by physicians, and it is logical for them to see death in such mechanistic terms. Important though such definitions are, and nowhere would we suggest that they are not important, it is our contention that previous definitions of death have overlooked the critical human component, that is, its social nature.

David Sudnow (1967) was among the first to establish empirically what we can call social death. In his study of a large metropolitan hospital, he found that morgue personnel studied lists of persons on "critical" lists to estimate work loads. The admissions office studied the same lists to facilitate the admission of new patients. Nurses on the ward and medical doctors making their rounds also frequently reacted to the nearly dead as if they were dead already.

Glaser and Strauss (1971) in another study noted that husbands and wives, parents, children, and others interacted with the dying in distinct ways. They might deny that death was even a remote possibility for the patient or they might talk in hushed voices; their reactions were distinct and highly patterned, different from ordinary, routine interactions. Because people reacted to the dying in distinct and similiar ways, the dying were conceived to occupy a status.

Building upon these and other earlier works, including nonempirical ones like *Catch-22* (Heller, 1952) with its character Doc Daneka, theorists began to argue that death for humans is most fundamentally social—the point at which personhood is lost.

The social dimension of death was forcibly communicated to Wallace (1973) when he was interviewing a woman whose husband had committed suicide. About a year before this man's suicide, he had suffered a massive stroke—one that left the fifty-two-year-old corporate executive and father of four reduced to a level of functioning that was less than that of his youngest child, who was eight. He could not work, watch television, read, or engage in other activities, however hard he tried. When he attempted to mow the lawn, "he made such a mess of it that he refused to even go outside again." After a year of such "life," he committed suicide.

When interviewed several months after the suicide, his widow said, "You know, my husband really died more than a year ago—when he had that stroke." The *person* who was her husband had indeed died at that time. Gone was the strong, decisive, energetic, and forceful person she knew as her husband and as the father of their children. From being almost totally submissive, the wife had had to become dominant, managing the family and its resources as her husband had once done. According to her own report, at the time of her husband's stroke she was "bereaved" at her loss. At first she refused to believe what had happened. Then she became angry, asking "Why?" Depression, guilt, and other typical grief reactions followed as the pattern set by the stroke became permanent.

Mrs. Burke, the name given her in the research, tried her loving best to care for her husband as he, too, struggled to accept the loss of his former life. When a year's therapies, medicine, and rehabilitation procedures failed to effect change, Mr. Burke added physical death to the social one that had already taken place. His wife again grieved, but her grief a year earlier had been by far the deeper one.

Examples such as the foregoing indicate the importance of the conception of death as social, but they are not the best evidence since physical death also took place, even though later. Therefore, the editors searched for a study of "pure" social death.

In an unpublished study completed at Columbia University, Lenore Weitzman studied what she calls "social suicide." In these cases, individuals feigned their own deaths, disappeared, and assumed new identities elsewhere. After investigations by an insurance company, which in fact provided Weitzman with the names of persons to interview, the "survivors" learned that those they had presumed to be dead had only died from *their* lives; they were very much alive to others.

In the survivors' reaction to social suicide, the impact of death as social can be clearly seen.

Social Suicide

Lenore J. Weitzman

Millions of Americans have committed social suicide. They have left home, disappeared, and never returned. More importantly they have abandoned their social identities. As physical suicides intentionally destroy their biological selves, these social suicides have intentionally destroyed their social or societal selves.

Social suicide is a sociologically rich phenomenon because it illuminates several central theoretical concerns. The phenomenon can be viewed in the context of identity strains in a mass society. Every status and role confronts its occupant with varying amounts of strain and conflict. Throughout our society people are faced with some problem or situation that they would like to escape. Perhaps not everyone truly wishes to escape, but it is probable that most entertain the idea from time to time. The theme of escape is widespread in American advertising, where a host of products promise that possibility.

Every person, no matter how pleasant one's identity seems to the outsider, feels that one's own strains and stresses are unique, even though they are commonly shared "problems." Every day people are faced with rising prices but the same income; with news of sickness or disease in their families; with conflicts of opinion with their spouses; with their inability to perform at work or in sports as well as they would like; with their lack of savings to afford the luxuries they would like or that their neighbors have; with fears that others are considered more worthy, brilliant, charming, attractive, or successful than they; with evidence of their failures as parents or their inability to influence their children; or with the rejection of their needs by others.

Given the universality of problems and the desire to escape from some of the pressures, disappointments, or frustrations in an identity, how are most people able to cope?

Identity Strain

Most people can cope with their identity strains by escaping part of the time. Others who define their problems as "severe" may solve them by relinquishing their marital, occupational, financial, national, religious, or organizational status. Both types of partial escape provide people with feelings of a change in identity or self-image. They remark, "I feel like a new person," "I've really changed since I last saw you," or "My whole life is different now that I am divorced." Thus, by temporarily escaping, as in a vacation, or by relinquishing a status, as in a divorce, the individual is able to relieve the identity strain while maintaining the continuity of a biography. For most people, social suicide is an unnecessarily extreme solution, and therefore it occurs infrequently.

Social suicide is also a rare event because it is a normatively deviant act. All of the normative or legitimate means of identity change provide a means of keeping track of and controlling individuals in society. The legal divorce is not just a means of record keeping; it is a procedure by which society can play a role in determining what happens to property and ensure that the children of a marriage will be provided for. Similarly, those who choose to change their financial status by declaring bankruptcy and those who choose to change their residential status by living abroad are regulated in their future behavior. In order to exercise social control over individuals, the society must be able to trace them and to hold them responsible for their pasts. By failing to maintain a continuous biography (and thus failing to be responsible for a past) the social suicide creates an identity that is nontraceable and therefore noncontrollable.

Three Types of Social Suicide

For many sociologists the term *suicide* itself is immediately associated with Durkheim's classic study of suicide (1951) as a socially patterned form of individual deviance. Durkheim isolated three forms of suicide—egoistic, anomic, and altruistic—and indicated how each represented a distinct form of individual integration in social groups.

We have similarly isolated three types of social suicide that represent distinct forms of individual integration in social groups. This typology will be used throughout because it distinguishes the patterns of social suicide with respect to the decision to leave, the mode of departure, the experiences after disappearance, the reactions of those left behind, and the individual's traceability by the locators.

Type I is the pure social suicide. It involves a rationally calculated and staged death that completely cuts the individual off from the individual's past and former identity. These individuals totally abandon their social selves—their personal identity kits, their occupational tools, their official credentials, their personal histories, and, most important, the symbolic representation of themselves—their names.

Type II is the drifters, who are distinguished by the gradual and partial nature of their identity changes. Many of the drifters do not completely abandon their pasts but retain parts of their former social selves.

The situational disappearance, Type III, falls somewhere between the total social suicide and the drifter. This type of disappearance is more abrupt than that of the drifter, and more of the social self is destroyed. The departure is more impulsive than the carefully planned pure social suicide. However, in departing, this type also abandons occupational, personal, and historical identities.

Each of the three types share the following features: they break away from their social anchorages, they fail to maintain a continuous biography, and they abandon a social identity. For purposes of this article, however, only Type I, the pure social suicide, will be discussed.

The Social Suicide

The following case histories are derived from two sources: the records of a large insurance company and the Family Location Service. The insurance sample includes all disappearance cases in the past ten years that were located by a company we shall call the Mutual Life Insurance Company. In all these forty cases, a person was presumed dead and a claim for policy benefits was filed with the insurance company. The Family Location Service sample includes all missing person cases that were completed by the agency in 1968. Interviews were conducted with twenty-five of the missing persons.

In addition to interviews with the social suicides, a great deal of time was spent talking to those left behind, friends and relatives of the missing (in both the old and the new identity), the locators working for the Family Location Service, the Mutual Insurance Company, private detectives, the police, and court officials. The files of the search organizations were also of considerable aid.

The author has called this type of disappearance a social suicide because, unlike the physical suicide, the person destroys only his *social* self. His body survives, and he continues to live after his "death."

Lars Holson Dr. Holson was one of the few professors at Ivy College who was swamped by students on Saturday nights. A jazz musician as well as a noted marine biologist, he often played at informal concerts in the International House on campus. Holson was especially concerned about foreign students and bent over backward to help them. His colleagues described him as a "one world humanitarian."

The assistant professor of marine biology had mentioned to several colleagues that he was anxious to drop some of his administrative tasks and spend more time on his research. His wife had also been told of his desire to devote more time to research and publishing, but she relied on him to help her with many household tasks. Holson was a skilled carpenter, and their cabinets and the boys' desks always seemed to need some work.

Greta Holson did not drive a car, and in suburban Rolling Hills this meant that her husband had to do most of the marketing and take her and the children to meetings. She was not interested in her husband's career; she knew little of and did not share his life on campus. And her objections to academic salaries were obvious to her husband and his colleagues. Yet she contended that she and Lars were very happily married.

When interviewed after her husband's disappearance, Greta Holson expressed her guilt over the fight that she had provoked the day he disappeared. She recalled that they were scheduled to take their youngest son for registration in kindergarten. They awoke early and got into the car to find that Lars had forgotten to fill the gas tank (after she had specifically reminded him the day before). They had to go in the opposite direction of the school to fill the tank before proceeding to the kindergarten. Lars was driving exceptionally fast, and they had an argument about his speeding and the way he was driving. After their son was registered, Lars dropped them off at home because he had an important meeting at the college at 10:30 A.M.

Mrs. Holson later found out that when he arrived his secretary told him the meeting had been canceled. He spent the morning in his office with some exam papers and left around noon for the bank. At the bank he paid the last installment on a loan they had taken out to cover the children's extensive medical bills and cashed a check for thirty dollars. After leaving the bank, he was never seen again.

His car was found near the bank, and both the loan book and the bank book were lying on the front seat. The bank he used was in a poor section of town, and the police admitted that a well-dressed man carrying a briefcase might be in some potential danger. The university and local police conducted a thorough search for Dr. Holson. Perhaps the strains of administrative and publishing pressures at school and the chores and the sick children at home had been too much for him. Perhaps he had committed suicide or had a nervous breakdown. Circulars describing the 6-foot-2-inch blond professor were distributed to every plane, train, and bus terminal in the area, to many other states in the U.S., as well as throughout Canada, Mexico, and the Caribbean.

Every mental institution in the surrounding area was checked, as were all of his former places of employment, his former residences, and past associates. Even pawnshops in the local metropolitan area were contacted, but to no avail. Eventually Holson was declared dead, and it was assumed that no one would ever know if he had been killed or had committed suicide. Mrs. Holson and her three sons moved, and she later remarried.

About the same time that Holson was declared dead in New York, he decided to leave his longshoreman's job on the Boston waterfront and apply for a job as a machine operator in a plastics factory. The job applicant who was seen by the personnel manager was a 6-foot-2-inch blond worker named Hans Sverra, whose new Social Security number and local address were dutifully recorded before he was sent down to work.

Vincent Montaro No one doubted the evidence of foul play the day that Vincent Montaro disappeared from his office in Tucson, Arizona. About noon that day Mrs. Montaro tried to call her husband to tell him that she planned to do some shopping, but the line was busy. Several subsequent attempts to contact him were also unsuccessful because of the busy phone. Finally, later in the afternoon, she began to feel uneasy that the phone was still busy. She stated it was not unusual for her to keep in close touch with her husband, calling him several times during the day about things, and since it was getting late in the afternoon and she had not heard from him, she decided to drive out and make a personal visit. Also, since he was in business for himself as a contractor, he came home early on afternoons when the work was slack, usually around 5 P.M. It was about 5 P.M. when she arrived at his office, and looking through the window, she noticed things were askew. Becoming alarmed, she called one of her husband's brothers, who was in town for the Christmas holidays. He arrived and surveyed the situation, finding a chair overturned, Vincent's glasses on the floor, his Catholic medallion near a broken ashtray, the office in a disheveled condition, and his billfold in an adjoining room. They called the police, who arrived about 6 P.M. Montaro's car was also missing but was later found in a nearby city.

The police immediately began to piece together the facts behind the mysterious disappearance of Vincent Montaro. He was a poor bookkeeper, but his construction business looked to be in order. His wife knew absolutely nothing of his business, so she hired a young lawyer to make a detailed audit of his accounts.

Kathy Montaro appeared desperately worried about her husband. She seemed genuinely to believe he never would have left voluntarily, and she assured the insurance investigator that they were very much in love, completely devoted to each other, and had two young sons who were a source of great pride and joy to Vincent. Neighbors confirmed a happy home life and successful construction business. Mr. Montaro was a model citizen; he had headed the church building drive and was considered a kind and charitable man.

The police sent out a thirteen-state bulletin and posted a local reward for any information leading to Montaro. Since his body had not been found, they suspected that he had been kidnapped.

A few days after the reward was announced, a former employee of Montaro's claimed that he had seen the missing man boarding a bus in a nearby community. The informer had been fired by Montaro for stealing on a delivery job, and no one gave his testimony credence. However, several days later the police reconsidered their hasty disregard of his story because the chief of police and Mrs. Montaro received a letter from another employee, who wrote:

> I done no harm to Mr. Vincent. Joe Daws and Earl Willison done him up and took his money. All I done was drive Mr. Vincent's auto and took nothing out and lefted it with the keys in by a filling station. Earl was wearing Mr. Vin's fancy watch. I don't know where they put him at. Joe and Earl took the $15,000 and they beat him out of his head with a stick. Earl said not to worry cause Mr. Vin was took care of good.
>
> I was suppose to meet them but they didn't show. I hunted them but they ain't here. All I say is I am sorry cause he give us all a job two years ago and was sure a real good boss man and we like him.

The letter came three weeks after the man disappeared. Authorities were contacted, but no further clues to Montaro's whereabouts were gleaned. After all, it would be difficult for the police, even if they made a thorough search of every building in the city, to know that a dishwasher, William Karsala, in a nearby city was the missing builder.

Features of the Social Suicide

Let us define the social suicide more precisely now that some of the case material has been reviewed. The social suicide is an event wherein a person disappears under circumstances which lead others to believe that the person has died. The individual's death is arranged by a serious accident or by a verbal or written notification of an intention to commit suicide. The social suicide is rationally calculated, carefully planned, and staged as a performance.

Some of the identifiable features of the male social suicide are as follows:

1. The first characteristic is the absence of any dramatic argument or crisis preceding the disappearance. Before departure, the lives of the about-to-disappear persons were carried on with regularity and normality. To the observer—even to their most intimate associates, their spouses and families—they appeared to be fairly happy in life. There were no fights or quarrels immediately before their departures.

With the exception of Holson, who argued with his wife the morning he left, eleven of the twelve social suicides did not leave after a specific crisis. Although another social suicide had had a brief fight with his wife before he left, he purposely provoked this disagreement so that he could storm out of the house in time to board a plane with his paramour.

2. The second characteristic is the surprised reaction of the wife. The women all expressed shock and dismay at the suggestion of suicide or even a voluntary disappearance. This goes beyond an unwillingness to face the negative elements in their married lives. Most of the wives vigorously asserted that their homes were happy and that their husbands had no reasons to want to leave.

3. The third distinctive characteristic is the wives' ignorance about their husbands' activities, especially the economic ones. It is hard to say how prevalent this is in American society, but with remarkable frequency the wives in this sample said they knew nothing about their husbands' day-to-day activities.

4. The social suicide may also be distinguished by what he chooses to leave behind. None of these men took any personal belongings, clothes, grooming aids, a pipe, or a favorite sweater. In Goffman's terms, they left behind their identity kits. According to Goffman, the identity kit consists of those items the individual needs for the management of his personal front:

> The individual ordinarily expects to exert some control over the guise in which he appears before others. For this he needs cosmetic and clothing supplies, tools for applying, arranging, and repairing them . . . and access to declaration specialists such as barbers and clothiers. (Goffman, 1959:88)

Although the form of their departures in part necessitated their need to leave their belongings behind, the failure to take any part of their identity kits was also indicative of their symbolic leave-taking with their former identities. As they were no longer going to be the same people, they no longer needed things that belonged to those persons' identities.

5. In addition, they left behind the tools of their trades. Some teachers left their education degrees and credentials—barring a future in their profession of teaching in a high school or university. Others left without any of the letters of credit necessary for a businessman to reestablish himself in a place where he is not known. A physician left without his license to practice medicine, his diploma, and his specialty board's certification—barring himself from practicing medicine in another community. Similarly, two men left without their union cards—effectively cutting themselves off from using the skills they had as well as from any seniority they had accumulated.

6. In addition to abandoning their personal identity kits and their occupational tools, the social suicides left behind the credentials that certify one as a member of our society: their birth certificates, driver's licenses, draft cards or army release papers, Social Security cards, credit cards, library cards, business cards, personal checks, and the myriad of personal identification papers that one accumulates to pass, pay, or be "socially processed." Thus they abandoned their official identities as well as their personal and occupational ones.

7. Perhaps the most significant possession abandoned by the social suicides is something less concrete: their names. With their names they left behind the sum total of their social selves. Thus they symbolically destroyed their social selves as well as their physical selves. Although they staged fake deaths, it would not be fallacious to say that on the day of disappearance, they did, in fact, cease to exist.

8. The eighth significant trait of the social suicide is the forethought that went into the disappearance. Each of these persons carefully considered their current situations and alternative courses of action. They calculated the costs of the alternatives and decided that a faked death and a disappearance were the best solutions to their difficulties. Great amounts of time and energy were spent in carefully planning their staged deaths. Each of them had to ensure that their actions before the disappearance were not suspicious. They had to routinely order their lives while planning their exits so that no one would suspect that they had consciously decided to leave. They had to calculate the time it would take them to get away to ensure that they would be safely hidden by the time their absence was noted. The extent of their planning is indicated by the amount of cash each managed to secure before he left. The one thing they did take with them, depending on their means, was money. If we carefully traced their activities before leaving, we would observe several visits to the bank to withdraw some money from their savings accounts or safe-deposit boxes. Only Lars Holson seems to have left without a sizable amount of cash; yet he was last seen at the bank cashing a check for thirty dollars, indicating that he was not completely oblivious to money.

9. Each of the deaths was staged well enough to be convincing. Each was reported to or discovered by the police and resulted in a police investigation that failed to find a missing body or the person.

10. Finally, in leaving, each of the social suicides left behind a past or a personal history. The unique biography that traced his life line, past doings, achievements, failures, and the "events" in his life died with the fake death. From that time on, the social suicide could not claim the history as his, nor could he claim the events and experiences as having happened to him. Thus, in this final break with his former self, he was left without a past.

Reactions of the Survivors

Having examined the general identifying features of the male social suicide, let us turn to an examination of how the female "survivors" reacted to the social suicide.

Fred West Mrs. West, an emotional woman, was dazed by her husband's accidental drowning. She blamed herself for letting him go fishing when he should have stayed home and continued to rest after his heart attack. Her oldest son was recalled from Vietnam because of his father's death, and the funeral was held immediately after his return home.

A lawyer was hired to help Mrs. West go over her husband's estate. Mr. West had left her deeds to all the property, but none of them were properly notarized. She cooperated with the investigation of the drowning by the local sheriff and the coast guard and assumed, as they did, that the body did not rise because her husband had drowned in a crab bed and the body probably had decomposed.

Mrs. West's real shock occurred after her husband's funeral. She discovered that he was married to another woman as well, and she now had to face a competing claim to Social Security and Veterans Administration benefits. She and her minister tried to keep her husband's bigamy a secret to save her further embarrassment in their home town. She was left grieving and bewildered by the turn of events.

The dominant reactions of the survivors are as follows:

1. The women reacted emotionally—with shock, dismay, grief, and the despair that accompanies any unexpected death. It is important to repeat that these women were responding to a death, not a disappearance. They all appeared sorrowful and displayed the usual signs of grief and mourning. There was, of course, a range of grief behavior among the wives and some variation in the degree of bereavement (Wallace, 1973).

2. They turned to family, friends, and clergy for emotional support. Often the surviving spouse asked someone else to handle the funeral arrangements for her.

3. They did not turn to the police or any other official agency; they notified their lawyers and the insurance company of the deaths. The survivors notified the insurance company so that they could receive the death benefits they were due; the wives sought their lawyers for help with the estate. Some women later applied for Social Security as well.

4. They were annoyed at the interference of the police and others. Some of the women were irritated with any interference because it seemed disrespectful, especially so soon after their husbands' deaths. As Sudnow has indicated, "Bereaved persons are regarded as persons with whom it is improper to engage in social conversation. . . . they are regarded as one for whom appropriate talk is to be restricted to . . . the clearly delimited structure of sympathy engagements" (1967:88).

Other women did not want the police asking too many questions because they did not want the authorities to discover embarrassing information to discredit their husbands. Two women were especially sensitive about their husbands' recent affairs. Another seemed to sense that there might be some irregularities in her husband's financial books.

The other wives of apparent suicides may have been intimidated by questions and felt the police were attributing their husbands' deaths to some fault of their own. This is especially true in one case in which the police felt the wife's behavior was suspicious because she would not answer their questions about her marriage and background. Many women simply felt the police were asking too many inappropriate personal questions.

Finally, the suggestion by the police that their husbands might have left voluntarily was regarded as an insult by the assumed widows, one of whom wanted to throw the police out of her house.

In two of the cases, police help was welcomed. The boss of one man did not know how to go about finding him or his body, and he was thankful for their expertise. Similarly, one wife (Mrs. Montaro) welcomed the police effort to find her husband, since no one was sure if he had been killed or just beaten up and kidnapped.

The reluctance of some wives to talk to the police can be easily understood. An investigation means digging into a host of personal affairs that most would prefer to keep private. Once the police come in, they have license to dig for information – and most people have what they consider skeletons somewhere in their closets.

5. Some of the wives felt guilty and responsible for their husbands' deaths. The natural reaction to news of the death of a close relative is remorse. However, guilt is also a common reaction, espe-

cially in suicide; one inevitably feels responsible for not having prevented the death.

In James Henslin's study (1977) of the reactions to suicide, he noted that his respondents tried to reconstruct their own interactions with the deceased and wondered if "I could have done something to cause him to do such a thing." Henslin went on to state that there are probably any number of routine interactions between people such that if one suicides, the other can interpret his part of the interaction as causal concerning the death. The result is guilt feelings that the person must contend with.

Mrs. Holson and another woman had had arguments with their husbands before they left and thus felt some guilt for their deaths; other wives felt responsible because of the marital tension in the home and assumed that if they had been kinder and more considerate the deaths may not have occurred; Mrs. West felt responsible for letting her husband go out after his illness. Only Mrs. Montaro and two other women appeared completely bewildered and in no way responsible for what had happened. They seemed very disturbed by the possibility of their husbands' deaths.

It is important to stress that the four women who felt guilty because there had been some marital tension were probably overreacting to the death and expressing universal feelings of guilt. Each said that she felt her husband was basically happy, and she knew of no reason why he would want to leave or commit suicide.

6. Most of the women were surprised and dismayed by the discovery of discrediting information about their husbands. For eight of the twelve women, the news of their husbands' deaths was soon compounded by the news of their financial insolvency and the resulting difficulties this entailed. Because each had a house, they did have some financial security. Yet these women had been married to men who were comfortable economically, and seven of the eight had never worried about money during their marriage. (Their husbands' incomes ranged roughly from $10,000 to $75,000 a year.)

7. The news of a possible voluntary disappearance left these women in a state of economic and emotional crisis. In most cases the women were subjected to a triple jolt: the death itself; the embarrassing discoveries about extramarital affairs and financial mis-

management; and the news from the police that their husbands' bodies had not been found. Each learned that there were suspicious aspects in the case and that possibly her husband was not dead but had voluntarily disappeared. When the insurance companies also informed them that their claims could not immediately be honored because of the possibility of disappearance, they were completely distraught.

It is important to emphasize that most of the women did not accept the suggestion of voluntary disappearance. They were annoyed and skeptical of the police or insurance investigators who raised this question, and most of them vigorously denied that their husbands could have done such a thing.

Their violent reactions to the suggestion of voluntary disappearance seem more realistically explained as annoyance at not receiving the insurance money they expected than consideration of the merits of the suggestion. For all ostensible purposes, most of the women continued to conduct themselves as widows. The extended insurance investigation was the final crisis they were forced to face within a period of a few weeks.

It is ironic that the men who "committed" social suicide were confident that their wives would be well provided for when they cashed in on their insurance policies. Like Willy Loman, who wrecked his car in Arthur Miller's *Death of a Salesman,* many of the men felt they would be of more value "dead" than alive.

Only two women took jobs. Another two eventually remarried.

8. Most persisted in the belief that their husbands had died and made no attempt to locate them.

In summation, the women left behind after a social suicide regard themselves as widows. They are often forced to confront discrediting information about their husbands and to cooperate with annoying and probing interviews by police. Most go through both an emotional and economic crisis and find themselves in more dire financial circumstances than they could have anticipated. Although every woman in the sample was a beneficiary of an insurance policy payable upon the death of her husband, none has yet received this payment.

Ω

Suicide After Social Death

Weitzman's study indicates that feigned death is real for those left behind. Had Weitzman been able to interview those who had feigned suicide, she probably would have found their deaths to be real and irreversible for them too. How could they return to those whom they had left? The survivors who learned the deaths were feigned also found them irreversible: "For all ostensible purposes, most of the women continued to conduct themselves as widows."

Death is social, and the social suicide examined by Weitzman documents our observation. Communicate to another that you wish to die from his or her life and that person will treat you as if you are dead. The persons the survivors knew did indeed die in social suicide and those human beings as persona are dead, although their bodies live on with different persona.

We have argued that because death is social, when the persona dies from our lives, death has in effect taken place. Even though the individual may be living a new life among others, to us he or she is dead. And even though we later learn of the person's survival elsewhere, our grief persists. We continue to feel bereaved.

In social suicide we examined cases in which a person who was another's husband or other relative — what we are calling persona — died, but the body lived on in a new persona. What about cases in which the body can no longer sustain the persona? We lose an arm or a leg and find that no longer are we a basketball player or a jogger. Or perhaps, as with Mr. Burke, a stroke makes it impossible for us to be employee, provider, doer, decision maker, or even conversationalist. Can we not say in such cases that the persona has died—that social death has occurred but the body lives on? And if we allow that social death has taken place, what then does willful death symbolize? Some cancer patients are among those for whom death is first social.

Suicide among Cancer Patients*

Bruce L. Danto

Cancer continues to be one of this country's major illnesses and causes of death. Perhaps it is for that reason that so little research has been conducted concerning suicide among cancer patients. Tragically, perhaps even among those in the healing arts, there is a subtle and underlying attitude of "Who cares; they're going to die anyhow." All too few are concerned about terminally ill cancer patients, especially about their psychological (Danto, 1973) problems.

In Schorer's (1961) review of the psychopathology of cancer patients, he noted their multifaceted denial. Reiser (1966) further explored the relationship between the psyche and the body, and the role of emotions in possibly causing cancer. Neither author acknowledged suicide as a possible reaction, although both were cognizant of the role of depression.

Farberow and his associates in a Veterans Administration study (1971) found that psychiatric patients had a suicide rate of 72.0 per 100,000 for the period 1959–66, whereas the rate for general medical and surgical patients in hospital settings for the same period was 6.0 per 100,000. Among those over fifty years of age in the suicide group, medical diagnoses were more common than psychiatric

*Significantly revised version of "Der Kranke im Endstadium: Selbstmord und seine Bewaltigung," in *Suizid und Euthanasie*, ed. Albin Eser (Stuttgart: Enke, 1976).

ones. The method of suicide differed between inpatients and outpatients. Among inpatients, 61 percent chose jumping, whereas 16 percent chose hanging and 14 percent cutting. Outpatients or those on leave from the hospital chose firearms in 52 percent of the cases and poisoning in 17 percent of the cases.

For those who were inpatients, the diagnoses were psychiatric in 68.6 percent of the cases, with psychoses predominant. In the general medical and surgical cases, neoplasms were present in 23.4 percent of the cases. There were about twenty different primary sites of the neoplasms, the most common being brain, face, pancreas, lungs, larynx, and tongue.

Achté et al. (1963) studied the incidence of suicide among cancer patients in Finland from 1954 to 1958 and found that 0.8 percent of all suicides involved people suffering from cancer. In another study Achté and Vaukonen (1966) found that 3 of the 32 patients committing suicide in nonpsychiatric hospitals in Helsinki suffered from cancer. Litin (1960) felt that suicide for cancer patients was not higher than normal, and Baltrusch et al. (1964) felt that suicide rates were lower among cancer patients than among the general population. Sainsbury (1956) found that cancer occurred twenty times more frequently among those who had committed suicide when compared to the general population.

In a recent research project Achté and Vaukonen (1971) studied suicides committed in nonpsychiatric hospitals in Helsinki during the period 1953–63. Within that decade there were 32 suicides, but only 25 could be studied because of missing records and other problems. Of the studied group, 14 were from forty to sixty-nine years of age; there were 15 men and 10 women; 10 were married, 5 widowed, 6 unmarried, and 4 had undetermined marital status. In all 10 cases of surgical patients, the suicide method involved was jumping. All the suicides had had previous histories of psychiatric symptoms, and psychoses were common. Of the 25 patients, 8 suffered from cancer. In the cancer group of patients, all suffered from depression. Two chose hanging, one gassed himself, and the rest chose jumping as their suicide method. In 12 cases suicide occurred within the first ten days of admission, and 18 patients killed themselves less than one month after their admission.

Dorpat, Anderson, and Ripley (1968) studied the broad relationship between physical illness and attempted as well as committed suicide. They selected the suicides that occurred during a twelve-month period in King County, Washington. In all there were 80 committed suicide cases available for study. They found that all patients had experienced physical symptoms during the year preceding their suicidal behavior, and 56 people had suffered from one or more diseases at the time of suicide. In 41 cases physical disease was believed to have contributed to the suicides. Nearly all the diseases were chronic, and 6 patients had suffered from malignancies. The study also included 58 cases of attempted suicide. In 20 of the cases, the subjects were physically ill at the time of their suicidal behavior.

Those who committed suicide were most likely to be over sixty years of age, and physical illness was the most common precipitating factor. However, the same causal relationship to physical illness did not hold true for the group who attempted suicide. In the suicide group there were more males who had suffered from physical illnesses. Eleven subjects had experienced surgery within the year before their suicides, and the surgery was considered to have played a major role in their deaths. In the group who attempted suicide, only 7 had undergone surgery a year before their suicidal behavior. For those who made serious attempts, surgery played more of a role than for those who made suicide gestures.

In the suicide group one-third were psychotic, and 30 percent suffered from some degree of alcoholism. Fear of death was common, and intense concern over chronic pain as well as altered physical structure and bodily function was also expressed. Many experienced significant shifts in their social relationships. Loss of a loved one was found to be a factor that precipitated suicide.

Of particular interest was the observation that 17 suicides died at their own hand to escape from their severe and morbid fear of contracting or developing cancer. Some researchers have argued that the suicides may have wanted to "master" death by some active means like suicide rather than contend with the possible prolonged waiting and uncertainty of a cancerous disease.

By contrast, Stenback (1972) argued that hypochondriasis is a defense against suicide because it prevents the need to destroy the body by punishing it through a morbid fear—punishing it but not destroying it — and working to preserve the body because of the fear of its loss.

Stewart (1957) found a high incidence of organic disease being omitted from death certificate recordings in cases in which the cause of death was suicide. In his series of 65 cases, there were 19 cases in which some form of organic disease was present, including 2 cases of cancer. He concluded that many more suicides might have had cancer or other forms of organic disease that played a causative role but that, once the determination of suicide had been made, such information was overlooked or omitted because it was considered unimportant. Three years later (1960) he reported the findings based on a study of 122 cases and concluded that organic disease incidental to suicide was even more common. Hypertension, in this series, was the most common organic condition found.

Farberow et al. (1963) studied a group of noncancer patients, ones suffering from cardiorespiratory disease, who had been treated at hospitals. The data for this group are of interest because they do not vary much from those of Farberow's cancer patients. The most common method of suicide for the cardiorespiratory group was jumping. Cutting and hanging were the next most common. A few shot themselves, and one used a can of hydrogen cyanide gas. None used any oral medication or psychopharmacologic agents. Farberow et al. also found that in their 32 cases of suicide among cancer patients methods of jumping and cutting accounted for 17 cases. The remainder involved shooting (4), hanging (2), poisoning (2), and setting fire to oneself (1). The method was unknown for the balance, but there were no known cases of medication overdose. Thus, a search of available literature about suicide among cancer patients fails to reveal any reports of suicide by tranquilizer or other medication overdose. The latter fact is significant in light of what is known about methods of suicide for the general population.

What is known about the population of cancer patients most likely to commit suicide? Again, there is little meaningful information available. Farberow (1963) described the population of his study as being surprisingly young; 34 percent were under forty-five years, 34 percent were between forty-five and sixty-four years, and 32 percent were over sixty-five. There were 19 Protestants, 9 Catholics, and 4 Jews in the total population of 32 cases. Lymphatic and hemapoietic cancers made up the major types of cancers for the younger group. Twenty-nine were listed as critical, and the others showed less severity. Of particular interest is the fact that in 15 of the 32 cases, the patient had reached a terminal state at the time suicide was committed. Some were in either oxygen tents or Stryker frames at the time they committed suicide.

As a type, the suicidal cancer patients were controlling, demanding people who wanted to direct their treatments. They were not liked by the hospital staff, and psychiatric consultations were frequent. They were clinically depressed about their illnesses and showed signs of depression, anxiety, apathy, and mood swings. They were married and experienced marital problems as well as pressures caused by the presence of preschool children at home and heavy financial difficulties. They showed a lowered tolerance to living with physical pain arising from a cancerous condition. Threatened or attempted suicide occurred in only 9 of the 32 cases. Of interest is the fact that confusion at the time of suicide was nonexistent.

Weisman (1974) observed that many cancer-treating physicians feel that suicide among cancer patients is high, but others claim that it is quite low. The fact is that little data have been gathered. Weisman concluded that in his experience cancer, like many chronic illnesses, creates many psychosocial problems, and some patients opt to terminate life. He felt that the relation between cancer and suicide increases if "the threat created by the cancer causes deep fears of dissolution, disintegration, and drastic changes in social roles." Social dissonance seems more important than does physical disfigurement and deterioration. After all, hope is a function of self-esteem; hopelessness means that one is unable to recognize or cope with insistent problems.

Ronald Koenig, a social worker at the University of Detroit who has had many years of experience working with cancer patients at Grace and Detroit general hospitals, discussed his observations in a private talk. In his experience patients with head and neck cancer have the highest suicide potentiality and performance, particularly in the time interval between diagnosis and treatment. They do not know where they are in relation to their deaths, and there are so many ups and downs in the course of their illnesses that they do not know the end point of their illnesses. If suicide occurs before a mental health referral can be made, the depression in many cancer patients is overlooked. Under treatment many cancer patients talk of suicide as a preferred death because it is predictable, unlike their illnesses, which deprive them of relationships to the future in terms of either life or death.

One of the reasons the depressed and suicidal condition of a cancer patient might be overlooked is that the traditional approach in medicine focuses on the disease and not on the person. During cancer therapy there are many physiologic and pharmacologic matters of concern. Most of the medical and nursing concern is directed toward those aspects of a patient's condition. Dubovsky (1978) pointed out that self-destructive behavior reflects the frustration and helplessness a patient feels when improvement is not on the way. This moment of human despair is frequently unseen by the physician who is struggling to save the patient's life or is trying at least to make the patient more comfortable.

No studies were found that dealt with fantasies of suicide or drug-induced suicide in particular, but it would seem that rescue fantasies are more common. Patients with chronic illnesses imagine the doctor discovering a miracle drug that will terminate suffering and cure the cause, namely, the illness. Thus, it is not so surprising that as the cancer condition courses toward a terminal state, the patient should sense, perhaps unconsciously, that the end is near, that the doctor has not found the magical cure. Perhaps the dying patient feels that some sense of dignity and self-determination can be achieved by choosing the time and place of death. Additionally, this patient may feel that suicide ensures a final expression of power and potency as a human being. Dubovsky, in agreement with this observation, stated that patients need to feel they control their lives. His cancer patients found that unless they could control their lives they would elect to die. For some of them death by suicide provided a feeling of mastery over their physicians. Dubovsky felt that if mastery could be supported in other ways, like having patients share in decision making, then suicidal thoughts and action would be alien.

Not all suicide is obvious. Nelson and Farberow (1976) studied 58 patients in an intermediary care unit of a Veterans Administration hospital by applying a scale designed to measure indirect life-threatening behavior. They felt that such behavior would throw light on a broader view of self-destructive behavior. All the patients had long-term illnesses of some kind, including cancer. The researchers were trying to find data concerning what was considered an indirect type of life-threatening behavior often observed on such wards. Such behavior leads to a person's premature death. It is associated with alcoholism, drug abuse, excessive obesity, reckless driving, victim-precipitated aggression, self-neglect, social withdrawal, and abuse of one's health. These behaviors are seen off the ward and outside the hospital setting among cancer patients who are being treated with radiation as outpatients. Inside the hospital patients may blatantly disregard their diets, smoke, expose themselves to drafts, be uncooperative about following treatment programs, or resist involvement in the treatment focus.

Farberow et al. (1971) found that patients who score high on the indirect life-threatening behavior scale also score high on suicide potential, have losses in many areas of function, have fewer social and material resources, are isolated and dependent upon an institutional environment, and have a low level of life satisfaction. They have high levels of dissatisfaction with staff members and ward and hospital activities and experience greater pain and discomfort in their illnesses. As a rule they are less religious than other patients, undergo longer periods of hospitalization, have lower senses of futurity than others, and feel more hopeless about life. They seem to seek out more risk-taking activities, are more psychologically rigid than others, turn to outside sources of control, and are more manipulative of others than most patients.

The results of this work are important to understand. They mean that self-destructive behavior is much broader than might appear to the average clinician and is more complex than suicide as viewed in the more traditional manner. This type of patient, actually passive because of depression, poses the additional risk of appearing to be compliant and might be seen by the medical staff as being a model patient. In that event the self-destructive behavior will be ignored.

Many physicians dealing with cancer would favor the idea of employing psychopharmacologic agents in the treatment of psychiatric problems of the terminally ill. Not only do such agents relieve both anxiety and depression, but they also potentiate the effect of narcotics and analgesics. Psychopharmacologic aids for the management of the emotional problems of cancer patients are no different from those used for the treatment of any depressed or disturbed person.

Since their introduction, tranquilizers have helped many people cope with otherwise paralyzing emotional changes. However, there have been limiting and even negative side effects. Physicians and nursing personnel too often bow to a philosophy of chemistry. Doctors make rounds of their patients by stopping at the nursing desk and writing orders. Patients receive more medication and less attention from their physicians, who rationalize that drugs are a time-saver and offer more to the patient than a quick visit. Psychopharmacologic agents take over and become encapsulated empathy as well as big business.

Recently, many clinicians have become disenchanted with psychopharmacologic agents. They have seen that such agents or tranquilizers do not hold up over long periods of time. The drugs are expensive, and a truly reliable and good antidepressant has not been devised. Fortunately, the need for people in the treatment program for the patient has become even more apparent.

Finally, some patients have used psychopharmacologic agents in suicide attempts or successful suicides. Psychopharmacologic agents have been relatively safe against suicide by overdose. However, deaths have been known to result from large quantities. Death can come about also because of other factors related to the overdose, such as cardiovascular complications like hypotensive collapse or the induction of such a degree of confusion that the patient loses control over various types of impulses like suicidal role acting. If liver metastasis is present, blood levels of ingested agents may be higher than normal due to failure to detoxify and even a moderate dose may become lethal. Many patients resent having to take so many pills and, in protest, discontinue taking prescribed medications. Patients do not want to feel more helpless and dependent than necessary.

Farberow et al. (1971) recommended more careful psychiatric screening of patients being considered for pass or discharge from a cancer ward. They found that telephone outreach with depressed patients and their families is beneficial. The researchers advised learning about possession of firearms as a part of knowing about the patient. In addition, patients should be removed from locations in the hospital where they might hang themselves. There should be protection against jumping from places such as high corridors and stairwells, and restraining screens could be added to the rooms housing depressed cancer patients. Patients must be assured that they will not be abandoned or permitted to suffer unduly. Farberow also outlined the need for suicidologic training of medical and surgical personnel as a prevention measure.

Craig and Abelhoff (1974) evaluated an instrument called the SCL-90, a self-report symptom inventory consisting of ninety items rated by the patient on a cancer ward. It clusters scores in terms of nine factors: somatization, obsessive compulsiveness, interpersonal sensitivity, depression, anxiety, hostility, probic anxiety, paranoid ideation, and psychoticism. This instrument was administered by nonpsychiatric personnel to thirty patients admitted to the oncology unit at Baltimore city hospitals from March through May 1972. The researchers found that 70 percent or more of the patients received scores under 1.0 on seven of the nine factors but that half of the patients reported scores of 1.0–2.0 or higher on the factors of depression and somatization. Knowledge of such elevated levels of depression might be useful in screening potential suicide in relationship to their degree of physical illness. Similarly, a high score on the obsessive-compulsive category might indicate a lowered suicide potential.

Experience has taught most clinicians who care for cancer patients that a professional relationship is essential, regardless of whether psychopharmacologic agents are used. How patients feel about their illnesses as well as what they fear about the future must be handled. Their families must be dealt with as well. In the hospital all personnel must be able to help patients come to terms with their conditions as well as to discover a sense of purpose for life even while in or approaching a terminal phase. Family and friends need leadership from the dying – their determination to make life meaningful and their interest in helping their families deal with illness and death. The family needs to know that they have done as much as is reasonable to help. Pills, liquids, and shots cannot accomplish these important missions. The patient and the family must be assisted by the staff to achieve such roles and relationships with one another. The patient must be helped to understand that suicide robs the person and loved ones of an opportunity to achieve that sense of purpose. Suicide for the survivors imposes the penalty of guilt feelings. A natural or nonsuicidal death helps the survivors more substantially.

Ω

Suicide, the Signature of Freedom?

Death is social. It is social for the survivor, and it is social for the suicide. As Danto indicated, at least some cancer patients, feeling loss of social functioning, choose death. "Social dissonance seems more important than does physical disfigurement and deterioration."

Aside from the fact that some commit suicide because they fear the loss of their persona – of who they see themselves to be – can suicide be defended on ethical and moral grounds?

As Fletcher said, social scientists can only "provide us with the data. . . . they cannot jump the gap between what is and what ought to be." Let us then turn from data to ethics. Death may be social, and suicide may symbolize the choice of death when the continued existence of the persona is questionable. Whether or not some may choose to end a life in which the persona has already died or is about to die, ought that to be the case? Let us first turn to Fletcher and then to Graber for possible moral and ethical justifications for what we already have established as empirical fact. Is suicide the signature of freedom?

In Defense of Suicide*

Joseph Fletcher

Most of us know that anthropologists have found every imaginable attitude toward suicide in both savage and civilized societies. Anthropologists, however, like psychiatrists and sociologists, are able only to provide us with data; in their scientific capacity they cannot jump the gap between what is and what ought to be. To suppose that tabulating moral sentiments described from observation settles an ethical question is what is called the naturalistic fallacy — confusing what is with what ought to be. Whether we ought to be free to end our lives or not is a question of philosophy, of ethics in particular. If a psychiatrist, for example, asserts or implies that people ought not to choose naughtness or oblivionate themselves (to use Herman Melville's neologisms), that scientist is wearing a philosopher's hat. *Ought* is not in the scientific lexicon.

In spite of the defiant immortalists who look forward to resurrection by cryonics or by outwitting cell death biochemically (such as Alan Harrington, who stated, "Death is an imposition on the human race, and no longer acceptable"), we know perfectly well that aging is a fatal disease and we all are its victims. The ethical question is whether we may ever rightly take any rational human initiative in death and dying or are, instead, obliged in conscience to look upon life and death fatalistically, as something that just has to happen to us willy-nilly.

We have pretty well settled the life-control issue with our contraceptive practices and policies; now we must look just as closely at the death-control problem. If we may initiate life, may we not terminate it? Were Ernest Hemingway and his father before him wrong to shoot themselves? Ethically? Psychologically?

The Ethical Question

Speaking as we are from the vantage point of moral philosophy, we must begin with the postulate that no action is intrinsically

*Translated from "In Verteidigung des Suizids," initially published in *Suizid und Euthanasie*, ed. Albin Eser (Stuttgart: Enke, 1976).

right or wrong, that nothing is inherently good or evil. Right and wrong, good and evil, desirable and undesirable—all are ethical terms and all are predicates, not properties. The moral "value" of any human act is always contingent, depending on the shape of the action in the situation—*Sitz im Leben* or *Situationsethik*. The variables and factors in each set of circumstances are the determinants of what ought to be done—not prefabricated generalizations or prescriptive rules. Clinical analysis and flexibility are indispensable. No "law" of conduct is always obliging; what we ought to do is whatever maximizes human well-being.

It is essential to grasp the difference between moral values and behavioral norms. Only in this way will we understand why our values are a priori while our actions should be flexibly selective and not legalistic or rule-bound. We might say that our opinions about what is good is subjective and visceral; our judgments about what we ought to do about what we feel is good are more objective and cerebral.

There simply is no way to "prove" our values by logic; they are established by a mixture of conditioning, choice, and commitment. As Ludwig Wittgenstein saw the problem, "This is a terrible business—just terrible. You can at best stammer when you talk of it."

On the other hand, when acting as moral agents, tailoring our deeds to fit our values and ideals, we have to use logic and critical reason, especially when we have to decide which value gets priority in cases of competing values. For example, if truth telling has a high-order value but conflicts with a therapeutic goal, telling the truth might sometimes be the wrong thing to do.

To suppose that we would always be obliged to follow any rule of conduct is only tenable on a metaphysical basis or because of an alleged revelation of eternal absolutes. Such universals are what the Greeks called the *proton pseudon*, the basic error of conventional (that is, unexamined) moralism. Most Christian and many Jewish moralists use starting points of this kind. Without such a supernatural support, however, any attempt to assign intrinsic moral value to anything—truth, chastity, property, health, or even life itself—is an abysmal ethical mistake.

Stepping for a moment into another context, we can clarify

the point at stake by quoting a question-and-answer column in a religious magazine: "Q. My wife is sterile but wants her 'marital rights.' I have a contagious venereal disease. May I wear a prophylactic sheath? *A.* No. Even though she could not conceive and you would infect her, contraceptive intercourse is an intrinsically evil act." The situation makes no difference. The end sought makes no difference. The good consequences make no difference. Nothing makes any difference. The act itself is wrong. This is the essence of "intrinsic" morality.

The typical moral theologian, for example, whose ethics prohibit suicide as such, would condemn a captured soldier's committing suicide to avoid betraying his comrades under torture — because suicide is held to be an evil act in itself, like Kant's *Ding-an-sich,* a defiance of the will of God. An empirical or clinical ethic, being without that kind of dogmatic sanction, would have to agree that suicide can be right sometimes, wrong sometimes.

A slight variant on saying "suicide is not right" is saying "we have no right" to end our lives by choice. People are always mixing human "rights" and right conduct together. In a humanistic ethics, when suicide helps human beings it is right. That is, we have a right to do it. What makes it right is human need. Human rights are not self-validating, not intrinsically valid. It is need that validates rights, not the other way around. When rights are asserted over or cut across human needs, we are faced with a set of superhuman moral principles that often can be callous and cruel contradictions of a humane morality.

Some History

William Shakespeare put the ethical question this way: "Then is it sin / To rush into the secret house of death / Ere death dare come to us?" *Anthony and Cleopatra* IV, XV:80–82. Cassio, though a good Catholic, thought Othello's suicide was noble. In *Romeo and Juliet* the priest did not condemn the self-conclusion chosen by the young lovers. Shakespeare never expressed the kind of moralistic horror we find in Dante, who put suicides in the Seventh Circle of Hell, lower than murderers and heretics. As a matter of fact, few cultures or traditions have condemned suicide out of whole cloth, indiscriminately.

Suicide poses an ethical issue that is ultimately a matter of values and how we reason about them. The story of what various people have thought and done about suicide does not settle the problem of what is right and good about it. Even so, the pages of history tell us things that help us to put the ethics of elective death in perspective, and we will look at the record in capsule.

Europe, Asia, Africa, America – all tell much the same story. Suicide is seen as absurd and tragic, noble and mean, brave and cowardly, sane and silly; every way of judging it has been taken. Some of the religious and the superstitious have condemned it wholesale; others have even praised it. For example, the Koran holds that suicide interferes with kismet, Allah's control of life and destiny, making it therefore much more to be condemned than homicide. Cardinal Richelieu expressed a similar idea. Some cultures, on the other hand, have honored suicides; the American Indians endured genocide at the hands of the Christian conquistadors Cortez and Pizarro even while their Spanish priests were condemning the Indians' selective suicide.

The Japanese honor the rite of seppuku, or hara-kiri, and the Hindu's honor suttee. Buddhist monks who used self-immolation to protest Thieu's dictatorship in South Vietnam are another example.

The Buddhist admiration for kamikaze is more complicated ethically because suicidal practices of that order combine killing oneself with killing others. Something like banzai is to be seen in the suicidal commando tactics of Palestinian guerrillas and in the "living bomb" gestures of Viet Cong terrorists. The supposed difference between committing suicide in banzai and volunteering to fly in the Luftwaffe or the RAF during the Battle of Britain poses an interesting analysis problem – speaking ethically, not psychiatrically.

More primitive peoples often believed that a suicide's soul or ghost would wander around without a resting place, haunting the living. To prevent this, medieval Christians buried a suicide with a stake through the heart and dug the grave at a crossroads instead of in "hallowed" (blessed) ground to keep it from poisoning the soil. The Baganda people used a similar defense strategy, as the storied missionary Livingstone discovered when he stayed among them. The Alabama Indians threw the bodies of suicides into a river; people in Dahomey threw them where they would become carrion. As often as culture groups made suicide taboo, however, others respected it or even revered it. In North American the Zuni frowned on it, but the Navajo and the Hopi did not; in the Pacific suicide was condemned in the Andaman Islands, praised in the Fijis.

The Bible never condemned suicide, although in later times the rabbinical Talmud did and the Christian church followed suit. Samson, Saul, Abimilech, Achitophel—their stories are told without censure. The term *suicide* itself only appeared in the seventeenth century. Not until the sixth century was the act proscribed; until that time, in the absence of biblical authority, condemnation of suicide had to be inferred from the sixth of the Ten Commandments, "Thou shalt not kill."

The Greeks were more judicious and therefore more selectively in favor of suicide than the Jews, and so were the Romans. Both the Stoics and the Epicureans approved it in principle. Zeno approved and so did Cleanthes. Seneca actually committed suicide, to forestall the murderous Nero's fun and games, and his wife Paulina joined him. On the other hand, the Pythagoreans, opponents of Hippocratic medicine, having their special knowledge of the god's decrees, opposed suicide because of what Islam later called kismet. (After all, if one "knows" what a transcendental and ultimate will forbids, one would be prudent not to do it.)

Plato allowed euthanasia, as Aristotle did, but in the manner of suicide, not in the manner of "letting a patient go." Homer and Euripides thought well of Jocasta committing suicide after she learned that her new husband Oedipus was her own son—which was, perhaps, an excessive and irrational reaction, but humanly understandable because of the strength of the incest taboo. The Romans, as we all know, allowed the *liber mori* for a great many reasons; they denied it only to criminals, soldiers, and slaves—for obvious military and economic reasons. Justinian's *Digest* spelled out the subject judiciously.

Christian Europe started moving from pagan Rome's compassionate regard for the dignity of free persons to the savagery of an indiscriminating condemnation of all suicide in the Middle Ages only after the Greco-Roman civilization had been ended by the Barbarian-Teutonic hordes. Once the classical philosophy was buried, the Catholic-medieval synthesis was able to take over, and one of its first major elements was an absolute taboo on suicide. In the manorial system nearly everybody was enfeoffed to somebody else; hence suicide was, in effect, a soldier's or a slave's unlawful escape from somebody's possession. It was fundamentally "subversive" of property rights.

The Christian moralists never put it that way, of course. Instead, they said that human life is a divine monopoly: "Our lives are God's." To take one's own life, therefore, is to invade Jesus Christ's property rights because he has saved us "and we are therefore his." This mystical theology was the bottom layer of the moral and canonical prohibition. It led some theologians to say that Judas Iscariot's suicide in remorse and despair was even more wicked than his earlier betrayal of Jesus and Jesus' consequent crucifixion.

A False Turning Point

St. Augustine marked the turning point in the hardening process. He was the first to make the prohibition absolute. None of the later antisuicide moralists improved on him; even Aquinas added only "It is unnatural," thus buttressing the theology with a religious metaphysics of "natural law."

We can outline Augustine's objections to any and all suicide in four propositions: (1) If we are innocent, we may not kill the innocent; if we are guilty, we may not take justice into our own hands. (2) The sixth commandment of the Decalogue forbids it, *non occides*; suicide is homicide; it is a felony, *felo de se*. (3) Our duty is to bear suffering with fortitude; to escape is to evade our role as soldiers of Christ. (4) Suicide is the worst sin; it precludes repentance; to do it in a state of grace (after one is saved, or cleansed of sin by Christ's blood) means one dies out of grace (unsaved, eternally lost or rejected). Augustine allowed an occasional exception for martyrs who had God's express directive or "guidance" to kill themselves; they were said to be acting as innocently as those who sin *ex ignorantia inculnata* (in invincible ignorance). This is the argument Augustine used to answer the Donatists, a Christian sect that pointed out that dying baptized in a state of grace, by one's own hand, was better than living long enough to fall back into sin, losing one's chance to have eternal life in heaven.

At the end of the Holy Roman hegemony, people began to reason again. By 1561 Thomas More (the "man for all seasons" who died for conscience' sake) had allowed suicide in his *Utopia*, even though Sir Thomas Browne frowned on it in his *Religio Medici* (1642). Montaigne backed More, and so it went. The great classic *coup de grâce* to the moral prohibition of suicide came with David Hume's essay *On Suicide* (1777), in which he reasoned that if suicide is wrong it must be because it offends God, one's neighbor, or one's self, and then showed how this would not always be true. Hume was joined by Voltaire, Rousseau, Montesquieu, and d'Halbach.

The conventional wisdom after nearly a thousand years of prohibition continued unchanged, as attempted suicides were hanged from the public gibbet. In Christian France, as in animist Dahomey, the bodies of the executed were thrown on garbage dumps. The properties of suicides were confiscated in England until 1870, and prison was the legal penalty for attempts until 1961.

At last, in the Suicide Act of 1961, England stopped making it a crime for a person, whether well or ill, to end his life or attempt to do so. There are only a few places left in the world where the courts are still trying to catch up to that kind of moral "sanity." Courts of law today are seldom as unethical about suicide as the conventional moralists continue to be.

Always and everywhere we find cultural variety and difference all along the spectrum of ethical opinion — from blanket prohibition to selective justification. In a very sane and discriminating fashion most communities, both savage and civilized, have believed that disposing of one's own life is like disposing of one's own property, that is, a personal election.

It is on this last ground that most governments in the West have been opposed to suicide. They have followed Aristotle and Plato, who contended pragmatically that except for grave reasons suicide seriously deprived the community of soldiers to defend it and workers to do its labor of head and hand. How weighty this objection is now, in an age of overpopulation, cybernated warfare, and automated industry, is an open question. In any case, the "right" to die is not right if and when it invades the well-being of others. On the other hand, when it is truly and only a personal choice, it is right. To deny this is to deny the integrity of persons, to reduce them to being only functions or appendages of systems of lords and seigneurs, or church and state.

Types of Suicides

Just as facts cannot tell us which things to value (although they may help) or how to rank them as priorities, neither can typologies. This caution applies, for example, to Emile Durkheim's famous classification of suicides into egoistic and altruistic, which is close to what we have come to mean in more recent days by "inner directed" and "other directed" – in the language of Riesman's *Lonely Crowd.*

Strong self-sustaining personalities are able (have the "ego strength") to defy cultural disapproval when or if a balance of pro-life and pro-death factors seems to weigh against going on living. As Albert Camus said, "Judging whether life is or is not worth living amounts to answering the fundamental question of philosophy." To drive home his point that philosophy is not merely impersonal abstraction, he added drily, "I have never seen anyone die for the ontological argument." There are times, although we may hope not often, when people find that the flame is no longer worth the candle. History and literature abound with instances.

Similarly, on the altruistic side, there are times when sacrificial love and loyalty may call on us for a tragic decision, to choose death for the sake of a wider good than self. The decision is made pragmatically, to promote the greater good or the lesser evil. An example is Captain Oates in the Antarctic snafu, who eliminated himself to speed up the escape of his companions; other instances are disabled grandparents pushing off on ice floes to relieve hungry Eskimos and brave men staying on the sinking *Titanic* or dropping off from overloaded lifeboats.

Durkheim had a third type of suicides, the anomic – those who suffer anomie, who have come to despair for either subjective reasons (including psychogenic illness) or objective reasons (maybe unemployability or outright social rejection). They reach a point where they cannot "care less." Demoralized, unnerved, disoriented, they throw in their remaining chips. One recalls Jeb Magruder telling the Senate Watergate committee, by way of self-excuse, that he had lost his "ethical compass." Suicide out of anomie or being normless, just as in cases when it is done out of ego strength or for loyalty reasons, may be rationally well-founded and prudent or may not. Suicides of all kinds, in any typology, can be wise or foolish.

This is perhaps the point at which to challenge directly and flatly the widespread assumption that "suicides are sick people, out of their gourds." This canard has lodged itself deeply even in the mental attitudes of physicians. It has managed to become the "conventional wisdom" of psychiatric medicine, partly, no doubt, because psychiatrists deal so much with false suicides whose verbal or nonverbal threats or "attempts" are signals of emotional or mental distress. Nevertheless, for all its persistence, the idea is basically silly.

Like universalized or absolutized moral norms, this one, too, is undiscriminating – a frequent diagnosis turned into a universalized stereotype. Some suicides are suffering from what Freud first called misplaced aggression and later thought to be diseased superego, but not all are. To say *all* is to be playing with universalized characterizations, and universals of any kind are fantasies, not empirical realities. (The hypocrisy of the courts has done a lot to encourage the dogma that suicides are unhinged.) The fact is that suicide sometimes can be psychiatrically discredited or sometimes can be ethically approved, depending on the case.

Those suicides who tell us about the fears and doubts that go through their minds are the "attempteds," not the successful and thorough ones, and the result is a marked bias or skew to the speculations and theories of therapists. Even more speculative are the ideas of writers who have lively imaginations (Thomas Mann, Boris Pasternak), especially when imagination is combined with a grasp of psychological jargon. Real suicides rarely leave any record and even more rarely explain themselves in any reflective detail; there are only a few exceptions like Arthur Schopenhauer, who thought suicide through but did not do it, and Sylvia Plath, who did. We only have to read Lael Wertenbaker's *Death of a Man* (1957), the story of her husband's noble and sane decision to cheat Big C, to get a more realistic appreciation of what suicide can be.

Suicide Today

In recent years the ethical issue about human initiatives in death and dying has been posed most poignantly for the common run of those in medical care, in the treatment of the terminally ill. Resuscitative techniques now compel them to decide when to stop preserving and supporting life; people no longer just die. What is called negative euthanasia, letting the patient die without any further struggle against it, is a daily event in hospitals. About 200,000 legally unenforceable "living wills" have been recorded, appealing to doctors, families, pastors, and lawyers to stop treatment at some balance point of pro-life, pro-death assessment.

What is called positive euthanasia—doing something to shorten or end life deliberately—is the form in which suicide is the question—as a voluntary, direct choice of death.

For a long time the Christian moralists have distinguished between negative or indirectly willed suicide, like not taking a place in one of the *Titanic*'s lifeboats, and positive or directly willed suicide, like jumping out of a lifeboat to make room for a fellow victim of a shipwreck. The moralists mean that we may choose to allow an evil by acts of omission but not to do an evil by acts of commission. The moralists contend that since all suicide is evil we may only "allow" it; we may not "do" it. The moralists do not mean that death is evil, only that dying is evil if it is done freely and directly by personal choice. Choosing to die is self-murder, just as a physician or friend helping you die at your earnest request would be guilty of murder.

Is it not ridiculous, however, to say that given the desirability of escape from this mortal coil or a tragic "crunch" in which one elects to give one's life for another value, all acts of omission to that end are licit, yet all acts of commission to the same end are wrong? Taboo thinking such as "all suicide is wrong" enlists false reasoning and invites inhumane consequences. The end or goal or purpose in both direct (positive) and indirect (negative) euthanasia is precisely the same—the end of the patient's life, release from pointless misery and dehumanizing loss of functions. The logic here is inexorable.

As Kant said, if we will the end we will the means, and if the means required is inordinate or disproportionate we give up the end. The old maxim of some religious thinkers was *finis sanctificat media.* Human acts of any kind, including suicide, depend for their ethical status on the proportion of good between the end sought and the means needed to accomplish it. Only if the means were inappropriate or too costly would the end have to be foregone. It follows that suicide is probably sometimes a fitting act and well worth doing.

How can it be right for a person to go over the cliff's edge helplessly blindfolded, while we stand by doing nothing to prevent it, but wrong if that person removes the blindfold and steps off with eyes open? It is naïve or obtuse to contend that if we choose to die slowly, forlornly, willy-nilly, by a natural disintegration from something like cancer or starvation, we have no complicity in our death and the death is not suicide; but if we deliberately our "quietus make with a bare bodkin," it is suicide. Every person's fight with death is lost before it begins. What makes the struggle worthwhile, therefore, cannot lie in the outcome. It lies in the dignity with which the fight is waged and the way it finds an end.

The summary principle is limpid clear: Not to do anything is a decision to act every bit as much as deciding to *do* what we would accomplish by "not" acting.

Consideration of suicide for social reasons (Durkheim's altruistic type) can easily lead to a philosophical debate about ethical egoism or self-interest *versus* social integration and utilitarian concern for the greatest good of the greatest number. Whether we limit our obligation to others to the parameters of enlightened self-interest or, more altruistically, of social solidarism, it still follows that we may be called to suicide for heroic or for sacrificial reasons. The fact that sometimes suicide subjects are unconsciously wanting to die anyway (Menninger 1938) is psychiatrically important but ethically irrelevant—unless, of course, we slide into the semantic swamp and assert that all who sacrifice their lives—parents, soldiers, police officers, researchers, explorers, or whoever—are sick.

More problematic and subtle than suicide for medical or social reasons are what we may call the personal cases. The ethical principle here is the integrity of persons and respect for their freedom.

Sometimes suicides act for profoundly personal, deeply private reasons. Often enough other people, even those close to the suicides, cannot add things up in the same way to justify the election of death. If there is no clear and countervailing injustice involved, however, surely the values of self-determination and liberty weigh in the suicide's favor. Social, physical, esthetic, and mental deficiencies, when combined, could weigh against the worth of a person's life. And who is to be the accountant or assessor if not the one whose death it is?

Conclusion

It appears that a basic issue is whether quality of life is more valuable than life *qua* life. And defense of suicide has to opt for quality, not quantity. The sacralists, those who invest life with a sacred entelechy of some kind, consequently make all direct control over life taboo. (We see this in the abortion debate as well as in the question of suicide.)

This question, whether we may act on a quality-of-life ethic or must go on with the medieval sanctity-of-life ethic, runs through nearly every problem in the field of biomedical policy—genetics, transplants, the determination of death, allocation of scarce treatment resources, management of the dying patient, human experimentation, fetal research, nearly everything.

Quality concern requires us to reorder values; those who promptly and dogmatically put being alive as the first-order value need to reappraise their ethics. One's life is a value to be perceived in relation to other values. At best it is only *primus inter pares*. Without life other things are of no value to us, but by the same token without other things life may be of no value to us. In *The Tyranny of Survival* Daniel Callahan puts it succinctly: "Unlike other animals, human beings are consciously able to kill themselves by suicide; some people choose to die." They want more than "mere survival," he thinks. "Models which work with ants do not work well when extrapolated to human beings."

The reason for this, we can add, is that human beings, unlike purely instinctual creatures, do not regard life as an end in itself. Life, to be up to human standards, has to integrate a number of other values to make it worth our while. Human beings can choose to die not only for reasons of love and loyalty but just because life happens to be too sour or bare. In Sean O'Casey's words, a time may come when laughter is no longer a weapon against evil.

The ethical problem, how to make value choices, comes down, as we have seen, to whether we reason with or without absolutes of right and wrong. Bayet back in 1922 had his own way of putting it in *Le Suicide et la Morale*. He said there are two kinds of approaches: an ethic of a priori rules and taboos or universal prohibitions or, alternatively, a "*morale nuancee*," an ethic rooted in variables and discrimination, that judges acts by their consequences, a posteriori. This essay is built on moral nuances.

Socrates and Karl Jaspers, 2,300 years apart, thought that the business of philosophy is to prepare us for death. Religionists, in their own way, have taken hold of that task; they have coped by a denial maneuver and a counterassertion of eternal life. Philosophers have ignored the problem for the most part. A good start was made with Epictetus' dictum: "When I am, death is not. When death is, I am not. Therefore we can never have anything to do with death. Why fear it?" Or take, in present-day terms, Camus' opening remark in his absurd essay *The Myth of Sisyphus*, that there is "but one truly serious philosophical problem, and that is suicide."

We have a striking paradigm for the ethics of suicide. In his *Notebooks 1914–16* Wittgenstein says that suicide is the "elementary sin"—blandly assuming, in tyro fashion, that survival is the highest good, even though it is individually impossible and corporately improbable that experience will bear this assumption out. Only on that unacknowledged premise was he able to say that "if anything is not allowed then suicide is not allowed." But then his superb mind forced him to ask, in conclusion, "Or is even suicide in itself neither good nor evil?" There, in a phrase, is the whole point ethically. Nothing in itself is either good or evil, neither life nor death. Quality is always extrinsic and contingent.

The full circle is being drawn. In classical times suicide was a tragic option, for human dignity's sake. Then for centuries it was a sin. Then it became a crime. Then a sickness. Soon it will become a choice again. Suicide is the signature of freedom.

The Rationality of Suicide

Glenn C. Graber

All of us mastered the use of the concept of suicide in the course of learning our native language. We know that certain deaths are appropriately classified as suicides (for example, the deaths of Romeo, Juliet, Ernest Hemingway), whereas certain others are clearly not suicides (for example, the deaths of John F. Kennedy, Lyndon Johnson).* The difficulty comes when we try to classify them as we do.

What is Suicide?

Let us consider some cases that result in death in different ways:

A. Arnold is fired from his job, the only job for which his training and his interests equip him. Upon returning home to tell his wife, whom he loves dearly, he finds a note saying that she has left him for another man—in fact, the very man who has just been given his former job. As he lights the stove to fix himself a lonely dinner, it explodes and his expensive home burns to the ground—which reminds him that he has allowed the fire insurance to lapse. After thinking through his plight for several hours, he takes a pistol (the only item that survived the fire) and blows his brains out.

B. Bernice is whistling a merry tune as she washes dishes, but when she touches the switch to turn on the garbage disposal, she is electrocuted and dies.

C. Clyde has a song in his heart as he eats his breakfast, but when he takes a sip of his coffee (into which his wife has mixed a generous amount of strychnine), he slumps over dead.

*There are, of course, some borderline cases in which we are unsure, even after all the facts are clear, whether to call a death suicide (several such cases are noted below). An advantage of the technique of analysis employed herein is that it allows us to make use of the insights we gain from examining clear cases to decide whether these borderline cases are appropriately classified as suicides.

Case *A* clearly is a case of suicide. Cases *B* and *C*, just as clearly, are not. What precisely is the difference between them?

The reply that first comes to mind is to say that Arnold killed himself by his own action, whereas Bernice and Clyde were killed by somebody or something other than themselves. The trouble is that there is a wholly reasonable sense in which Bernice and Clyde can be said to have killed themselves by their own actions, too. After all, Bernice reached out her hand and touched the switch. The electricity did not come to her. (Contrast the case of someone struck by lightning.) And Clyde picked up the cup and drank from it. (Contrast someone who is held down and has poison injected into his veins.) Thus, the fact that one's death results from one's own action is not sufficient to qualify it as suicide. Some cases of accidental death (Bernice) and murder (Clyde) also have this feature.

What we need is to find some feature of the cases that distinguishes Arnold's action in relation to his death from the actions of Bernice and Clyde. One possibility is the difference between characteristic effects and unusual or uncharacteristic effects. This criterion would distinguish the cases cited so far in the proper way. To put a gun to one's temple and pull the trigger (as Arnold did) or to remain in a closed room in which gas is escaping as someone we will call Donna – Case *D* – did, characteristically causes death. In contrast, to put a cup of coffee to one's lips and drink does not characteristically cause death. It is only in the unusual circumstance in which there is poison in the coffee that a drink of it will kill. Bernice's death is likewise an uncharacteristic effect of her action, for it is only when something has gone wrong with the wiring (which is not the usual condition) that it will be a fatal act to touch a wall switch.

However, this criterion will not serve to distinguish suicide from other kinds of death in all cases. It is possible to commit suicide by means of abnormal or uncharacteristic conditions if we know about them in advance. If one knows, for example, that there is a short in a particular wall switch, then one could commit suicide by stepping into a bucket of water and then touching the switch. If Clyde had watched his wife pour the poison into his coffee and knew that it was poison but deliberately drank it anyway, we would judge that he committed suicide. In these cases, death is an uncharacteristic result of the action, but it is a suicide nevertheless. Hence we cannot define suicide in these terms.

These counterexamples suggest another possibility. Perhaps knowledge is the key to the distinction between suicide and other kinds of deaths. At least one theorist has thought so. The sociologist Emile Durkheim defined suicide as "all cases of death resulting directly or indirectly from a positive or negative act of the victim himself, which he knows will produce this result" (Durkheim, 1951:44).

This definition does not seem adequate. It does not distinguish between the two following cases, the first of which seems clearly to be suicide and the second of which seems equally clearly not to be.

E. Edgar is a wartime secret agent who is captured by the enemy. Knowing that he will be tortured mercilessly to the death, he takes a cyanide capsule from a hidden compartment in his shoe, bites into it, and dies.

F. Francine is another wartime secret agent who is captured. She has heard before about these particular captors and knows that they always torture to the death any agent who refuses to divulge the information they are after. Nevertheless, she refuses to tell them anything. After three painful days, she dies from their tortures.

The difference between these two cases is a subtle one, but since it is both real and important to the analysis of suicide, we will take time here to bring the difference into focus. In order to do this, we must note some preliminary points about the nature of action.

A single action has multiple effects. For example, Edgar's action not only has the consequence of bringing about his death but has the additional effects of guaranteeing that he does not divulge whatever strategic information he knows ("Dead men tell no tales") and of sparing him the pain of tortures that would otherwise be inflicted upon him. It may have still other effects as well. If we suppose (as is not unlikely) that one of Edgar's captors had been assigned the responsibility of searching captured agents in order to find concealed poisons and if the commanding officer is as ruthless as his procedures for treatment of captives suggest that he is, then Edgar's action of taking the poison may have the additional consequence of prompting the execution of one of his captors.

Some effects are causally independent of other effects. For example, consider the two consequences: Edgar's guaranteeing the protection of his secrets and his bringing about the execution of his captor who failed to find the poison. Neither of these is directly causally related to the other. The captor is executed, not because the secrets were successfully protected but because he failed to carry out an assigned responsibility. Imagine that Edgar had not succeeded in guaranteeing the protection of his secrets. Imagine, for example, that he had inadvertently left a written statement of them intact in his pocket. The chances are good that his captor would still have been executed. The fact that the soldier had failed to do his assigned duty would remain as the basis for punishment. Thus these two consequences are both effects of Edgar's swallowing the poison, but they are causally independent of each other.

Now we must consider the element of intention in action. Some of the effects of a given action are intended. More specifically, whatever goals the agent hoped or planned to achieve by performing the action are intended effects of the action. It is reasonable to assume that both Edgar and Francine had the same ultimate goal in mind in doing what they did; both wanted to protect the secret information in their possession. Thus this is clearly an intended effect of their respective actions. In addition, it is likely that Edgar was also influenced by the realization that death from the poison would spare him the pain of torture. Hence this can plausibly be interpreted as a second, coordinate goal of his action and thus another intended effect of it.

Some effects of an action are not intended effects. Consider the consequence of the execution of one of Edgar's captors who failed to find the concealed poison. Surely this was not an intended effect, and Edgar was probably not even aware of it. Of course, it is possible that he did know beyond reasonable doubt what would happen. Even if he knew, however, it would still seem a mistake to say that he intended for it to happen. Awareness of this consequence played no role at all in his decision to act as he did. His interest was in protecting his secret information in the best way he knew. The realization that an enemy soldier would die as a result of his action made him neither more nor less inclined to act. That consequence was, then, a by-product, a side-effect, or an incidental effect of his action, perhaps foreseen but not intended. This brings us to our final point about action: some of the effects of an action that are foreseen are nevertheless not intended effects.

It is important to establish this last point because it provides the key to the distinction between Edgar and Francine and, ultimately, the basis for criticism of Durkheim's definition of suicide. For Francine, her own death was a by-product or a side-effect of her action and not an intended effect. Her goal was to protect her secret information in the best way she knew—by remaining silent. She would have done the same thing if she had not known what her captors would do to her as a result or if she had known that they would *not* kill her, and her realization that these particular captors would surely kill her made her neither more nor less inclined to talk. (This may be too strong. She may have been tempted to talk in order to save her life, but she resisted the temptation and remained silent.) Thus her death was a foreseen but unintended consequence of her action.

Edgar's situation is importantly different from this. His death was not a side-effect of his action. Rather it was a part of the means he used to achieve the goal. His taking the poison caused his death, which in turn provided the guarantee that his secret information would be protected (assuming now that he remembered to destroy any notes).

The upshot of all this is that knowledge of the consequences is not what distinguishes suicide from nonsuicide, as Durkheim believed. Both Edgar and Francine knew that they were going to die. What makes the difference between suicide and nonsuicide is the intention of the agent. Edgar intended to die, and thus his death was suicide. Francine, in contrast, did not intend to die. Her death was a side-effect of her action, and thus she was not a suicide.

Now we have the key to the proper analysis of suicide. The crucial difference between suicide and other kinds of death is to be found in the intentions or purposes of the person who dies. This can be seen clearly in the cases discussed so far. Arnold, Donna, and Edgar (our three suicides) all did what they did with the express intention of bringing about their own deaths. Bernice, Clyde, and Francine, in contrast, had no such intention. Bernice was trying to get rid of the garbage. Clyde wanted to drink some coffee. Francine was interested in protecting the national security of her country. None of the nonsuicides acted with the intention of dying; all of the suicides did act as they did for this purpose.

Thus our suggestion passes the first test of adequacy for a proposed analysis. It matches our preanalytic judgment about what is suicide and what is not. The crucial difference between suicide and other kinds of death is to be found in the intentions or purposes of the person who dies.

However, there is still some work to be done. In the first place, we need to formulate the suggestion into an explicit analysis so that we can see more clearly precisely what it involves. One way of doing this is proposed by Joseph Margolis, who defines suicide as "the deliberate taking of one's life in order simply to end it, not instrumentally for any ulterior purpose" (Margolis, 1975:26). This description might fit the cases of Arnold and Donna. If someone had asked them, just prior to their acts, why they were preparing to take their lives, each might have answered by saying something like "My life is meaningless; I simply want to end it." This is the sort of thing Margolis has in mind.

However, Margolis' definition does not fit Case E—Edgar. If we had asked Edgar whether his purpose in taking the poison was simply to bring about his own death, he would undoubtedly have answered with a resounding "No!" He had two ulterior purposes: to protect his secrets and to prevent the pain of torture. If he could have found any way to reach these goals that did not involve his death, he would not have ended his life. For him death was a means or instrument to an ulterior purpose, not something he wanted in itself. And yet we have agreed that his death was suicide. Hence Margolis' proposal for a definition of suicide must be rejected, since it does not match our practical classifications in this sort of case.

Indeed, there is a plausible aspect in the cases of Arnold and Donna that would put even them outside Margolis' analysis. Suppose they explained their actions by saying, "I am in despair, and I want to end this awful anguish." The natural interpretation of this is to say that ending their anguish is for them an ulterior purpose to which their deaths are means or instruments. Then, on Margolis' analysis of suicide, we would have to say that these deaths are not suicides. Surely this is mistaken.

R.B. Brandt works intention into the analysis of suicide in a more promising way. He proposes the following definition:

> "Suicide" is conveniently defined, for our purposes, as doing something which results in one's death, either from the intention of ending one's life or the intention to bring about some other state of affairs (such as relief from pain) which one thinks it certain or highly probable can be achieved only by means of death or will produce death. (Brandt, 1975:363)

However, this analysis is too broad. By this definition, not only would Edgar's death qualify as suicide, but so would Francine's. Her goal is to protect her nation's secrets, but she is aware that it is highly probable that the same action that will achieve this purpose (that is, her negative action of remaining silent) will also produce her death, since it is the known practice of her captors to kill agents who remain silent. Yet we agreed earlier that Francine's death is not a suicide. Thus we cannot be satisfied with Brandt's definition as it stands. It is too close to Durkheim's definition.

We can produce an accurate analysis of suicide by amending Brandt's definition. It will not do simply to drop the whole phrase that reads: "or the intention to bring about some other state of affairs (such as relief from pain) which one thinks it certain or highly probable can be achieved only by means of death or will produce death." What would be left is equivalent to Margolis' definition, which we have already discarded as too narrow.

The analysis of suicide we want must include deaths (like Edgar's) that are intentionally brought about as a means to some ulterior purpose, and it must exclude deaths (like Francine's) that are foreseen but not intended consequences of deliberate actions. Actually, we can achieve this quite easily. All we have to do is to drop the last four words of Brandt's analysis: "or will produce death." It is this phrase that brings in deaths that are foreseen side-effects of deliberate actions.

Incorporating into Brandt's definition the two changes we have made, we get the following analysis of suicide: Suicide is defined as doing something that results in one's death in the way that was planned, either from the intention of ending one's life or the intention to bring about some other state of affairs (such as relief from pain) that one thinks it certain or highly probable can be achieved only by means of death.

Let us test this analysis further by examining its implications for certain additional cases. First, consider this pair of cases:

> G. Gary is in constant and intense pain caused by terminal cancer. Somehow he manages to get hold of a large quantity of a pain-killing drug, which he takes all at once, saying "I want to die. It is the only way to get rid of this awful pain."
>
> H. Helen's physical condition is just like Gary's. She takes the same amount of the same drug, but she says, "It is not my intent to die. I am taking this dosage because nothing less will completely relieve the pain and I am determined to get rid of the pain, even if it results in my death."

Our analysis compels us to say that Gary's death is suicide, but Helen's is not. (This assumes, as we must in the absence of explicit evidence to the contrary, that they both mean exactly what they say. The ultimate goal of the action in both cases is to be rid of pain. For Gary death is a means to this end, but for Helen death is a by-product of the means chosen (which is to take a dosage large enough to guarantee that it is effective in relieving the pain). There is another way of specifying the difference between these two cases. Helen might not be disappointed if she were to wake up a day or two later to find that the pain had returned. Not dying is compatible with (although not dictated by) her expressed motive that all she wants is temporary relief from the pain, a rest for a while from the burden. Gary, however, would react differently. If he were to come out of a coma a day or two later and still be racked with pain, he would be bound to feel that he had failed to accomplish his purpose.

There is one more implication of this analysis that should be brought to attention. We have said that the classification of an act as suicide hinges on the person's intentions or purposes. Psychologists tell us, however, that many people who attempt suicide do not really want to die. Their actions are really desperate calls for help from other people. Of course, some of them take a stronger action than they had intended, or the intervention they had expected does not come, and they do die. By our analysis, these are not actually suicides. They are accidental deaths. Thus our definition entails that what police agencies and others regard as the clearcut cases of suicide may not be suicides at all. Just because someone is found hanging from a rope he tied around his own neck or dead from a self-administered dose of sleeping pills, this does not prove that he committed suicide. It may not have been his intention to die.

Suicide and Rationality

Is suicide ever rationally justified? It seems clear that it sometimes is. Let us begin with a closer look at the situation of our old friend Edgar, the wartime secret agent.

His only choice is between death today and death tomorrow after incalculable pain, and surely he is correct in choosing the former option. It is the only rational decision in such a situation. Think first about his appraisal of the facts of the situation. He has reliable evidence that it is the practice of these captors to kill captured agents. He would be hoping against hope if he expected his captors suddenly to become soft-hearted and spare his life. It would be equally unrealistic for him to think that his compatriots would risk the success of their cause (as well as their own lives) to rescue him. He must face the fact: he is doomed.

Now consider his appraisal of the values. It would also be irrational not to want to avoid torture. The pain of it is reason enough to want to avoid it, but Edgar must also consider the very real risk that he might break under torture and betray his cause.

We acknowledge the rational justification of suicide in this sort of case, whether in fiction or in real life. Our usual emotional reaction is admiration for the agent for having the courage to follow what is obviously the only sensible course of action. (Note that we have not said he is morally justified. This is still an open question that we will consider shortly.)

Let us now step back from this example and see if any general principles can be abstracted from it. The way to get at such a principle is to ask, what is it about Edgar's situation that leads us to think that it is rationally justified for him to take his life? The answer to this question seems obvious. Once we are convinced that Edgar has not made any errors in his appraisal of either facts or values in the situation (which is one important aspect of rationality, but not the whole story), what persuades us of the correctness of his decision to kill himself is our own perception that he is better off dead. If we measure the advantages and disadvantages of both options open to him, it appears clear that the choice to kill himself immediately is likely to produce a greater total value (or, what amounts to the same thing, a lesser total disvalue) than the other option. This, then, is our general principle of rational justification in suicide. *It is rationally justified to kill oneself when a reasonable appraisal of the situation reveals that one is really better off dead.*

The best way to see whether the principle really works in practice is to try to apply it to some specific cases. Let us look, for example, at the situations of the cancer patients Gary and Helen. Each of them is racked with pain from an incurable and terminal illness. Gary decides to kill himself, and Helen chooses a course of action that results in her death. Are their decisions rationally justified? Only a short period of life is left to them anyway, and it will be filled with extreme pain. In this respect, their situations parallel Edgar's. It would be unreasonable of them to expect a sudden spontaneous remission of the disease at this advanced stage or to expect a miracle cure in the near future. There are some additional values open to them that are not available to Edgar. Whereas Edgar has only his hostile captors to keep him company, Gary and Helen are surrounded by more or less sympathetic people – including their families and close friends. The value of these contacts cannot be ignored, and their decisions would be unjustified if they left these values out of account altogether. Surely Gary and Helen are not being unreasonable, however, if they question whether the continuation of these human contacts is worth the cost in pain. The value of the benefits of which immediate death would rob them is outweighed by the disvalue of the pain from which death would spare them. Hence we must say that they would be better off dead and that ending their lives is therefore rationally justified.

Several points about this argument call for comment. First, the judgment that a certain person would be better off dead must be made entirely from that person's own point of view. The fact that Gary is an emotional and financial burden to his family is, in itself, totally irrelevant to the issue of whether he would be better off dead. It might be significant in saying that the family would be better off if he were dead, but that is another matter entirely. Of course, if Gary is aware that he is a burden, this awareness will be detrimental to his welfare. Awareness of being a burden, however, is different from the fact of being a burden, and only the former counts toward saying that he would be better off dead.

The second point is more complicated—and more controversial. We must acknowledge a person's own tastes and preferences, but we must not extend a blanket acceptance of all the value judgments of that person. If, for example, a woman prefers chocolate ice cream to pistachio, we cannot say she is mistaken, but if she prefers eating mud pies to eating ice cream, then surely she *is* mistaken about values. Objective values set the limits for legitimate and reasonable preferences. Among things that are of roughly equivalent value (for example, ice cream of different flavors, foods of different kinds of roughly equal nutritional value, styles of music, literature, or art), the choice between them is left entirely to the individual's taste, but if the value that the person places upon a thing (for example, mud pies) is too far out of line with its objective value, then the preference is labeled as unreasonable.

This principle is not limited in application only to trivial matters. The same value governs the choice of an occupation and a lifestyle. The choice between a career as a lawyer and one as a teacher is largely a matter of individual taste, but it would be unreasonable (economic considerations aside) for one to devote one's whole life to collecting odd bits of string.

The same reasoning applies in the case of Gary. We may feel that if we were in Gary's situation, we would rather endure the pain in order to be able to continue to enjoy association with other human beings. Nevertheless, if Gary himself is not afraid of death (with the resulting loss of human contacts) and prefers it to a continuation of the pain, we have no right to impose our preferences upon him by insisting that he is not rationally justified in ending his life. On the other hand, if Gary were to say that he saw no value at all in human associations or no disvalue at all in death, he would be mistaken and we ought not to endorse his mistaken judgment.

In other sorts of cases, it is much more difficult to form a judgment about the rationality of suicide. Let us look at one troublesome case:

> I. Irene used to be an especially active young woman. She was a professional dancer, and all her favorite avocations were strenuous physical activities like swimming and tennis. As the result of an automobile accident, she is now paralyzed from the waist down, and the functioning of her arms and hands is impaired. She decides to kill herself, saying, "I would be better off dead than living as an invalid."

Is her decision rationally justified?

It must be admitted that she faces something less than a full and complete life. She will never again be able to participate in the kinds of physical activities that mean so much to her (and also mean a great deal to many other people). Her life is diminished as a result of her accident. We acknowledge this when we speak of the accident as a misfortune or a tragedy and of its results as a loss.

However, a life thus diminished is not totally robbed of value. Irene still has a lot going for her. She has full use of her mental faculties, full ability to communicate, and partial mobility of arms and hands. She can maintain meaningful and satisfying relationships with other people, and if she put her mind to it, she could undoubtedly devise a number of projects within her capabilities with which to occupy her time. We all know of people who have managed to make satisfying lives for themselves in spite of handicaps even more severe than Irene's.

There is no guarantee that Irene will make a satisfying life for herself. We all also know of persons, some less severely handicapped than Irene, who have remained bitter about their losses and, as a result, have isolated themselves from others and refused to try to devise constructive ways to fill their time. It is hardly surprising to find that many of these people look back over their lives and judge that they would have been better off dead. A life of bitterness, isolation, and self-pity is not clearly superior to no life at all.

In the face of these conflicting possibilities, how are we to determine whether Irene's life is worth continuing? It is tempting to say that the judgment should be left entirely up to Irene. However, this is an evasion. Unless we are willing to aid her by constructing a set of rational criteria on which she can make her judgment, we will have done nothing but add the weight of responsibility to her already considerable burdens. Moreover, it is an open question whether she is in a better position to apply such criteria than is somebody else.

Another tempting response is to look to capabilities rather than to possibilities or probabilities as the basis for evaluating life prospects. We have said, for example, that Irene can maintain relationships and that she could devise projects. Whether she actually does any of these things is, presumably, up to her, but even if she fails to do them, the fact remains that she is capable of doing them. This might seem to be enough by itself to say that her prospective life is worth living.

The trouble is that it may not be within Irene's power to control whether she fulfills these capabilities. She may fight against bitterness only to find that she cannot prevent its setting in. She may actively try to devise projects to fill her time only to discover that she cannot develop an interest in any of them. How one reacts to a misfortune like Irene's is not decided by conscious choice or effort of will. It involves factors in the personality that have developed gradually over the whole of one's life and cannot be altered in any direct way. Irene's entire life has been oriented exclusively toward physical activities, and so she may not have any interest in or ability for the kind of quiet activities that are now her only hope. If she finds that these activities fail to satisfy her no matter how hard she tries to develop an interest in them, it would be neither surprising nor unreasonable for her to conclude that she would be better off dead.

There is one very important value that we have not yet considered in Irene's situation. In order to get at it, let us look at the following case.

> J. Jeremy is yet another secret agent who is captured, but his captors are very different from those who got hold of Edgar and Francine. Instead of brutal torture, these people go in for subtle and sophisticated techniques of brainwashing that render the subjects willing and eager to share any strategic information they happen to know. Jeremy knows of their methods, and he also knows (as a result of a battery of psychological tests that were taken in the course of his training) that he is highly susceptible to such influence. He bites a cyanide capsule because he does not

want to become the sort of person who would willingly betray his cause.

What this case brings out is the value of personal ideals and personal integrity. Jeremy has set certain ideals for the kind of person he wants to be; among other things, he wants to be loyal to his country. Departure from this ideal might not cause him any pain. If the brainwashing is totally effective, he might not feel any pangs of conscience when he betrays his country. He might even be proud of doing so because after the brainwashing is completed, he will have become a different kind of person than he is now—the kind whose loyalties are directed toward the cause of his captors. The trouble is that he does not now want to become the kind of person he would then be.

This is what is so insidious and frightening about techniques of brainwashing. They affect what is most dear to the victim. They alter one's ideals for the kind of person one wants to be and thus violate personal integrity. In an important sense, they destroy the *person* and put a different person in its place.

Irene might view her prospects in a way parallel to Jeremy's line of thought. She might be fairly sure that, in time, she could adjust to life as an invalid and find satisfaction in it. She can remember that she has enjoyed short periods in bed with minor illnesses, and she can imagine herself becoming totally engrossed in television soap operas, syrupy novels, and needlework. She also realizes that she finds a certain amount of pleasure in the pity and solicitude of those who come into contact with her, and she can imagine that this aspect of her nature will expand as time goes on.

However, she does not want to become this sort of person. She has always regarded this part of her nature as unworthy and has worked to suppress it, and the prospect of its becoming dominant in her personality is repugnant to her. She would rather end her life than to become this sort of person.

Some General Conclusions

In the course of this discussion, we have reached some general conclusions about the rationality of suicide. It might be helpful to repeat them in a list here:

1. Some suicides are rationally justified (Edgar and Gary, for example).

2. Some suicides are not rationally justified.

3. It is rationally justified to kill oneself if a reasonable appraisal of the situation reveals that one is really better off dead. This is the criterion of rational justification for suicides.

4. The judgment that a certain person is (or is not) better off dead should be justified exclusively:

a. From the person's own point of view;

b. Within limits, on the basis of the person's own tastes and preferences;

c. On the basis of actual preferences (present and future), rather than abstract capabilities.

5. The prospective suicide's judgment of whether he or she would be better off dead is not the last word on the matter. The person may be mistaken.

a. The person may make a wrong prediction about the degree to which his or her present values are likely to be satisfied. ("I'll never be able to keep up my career now that I am blind.")

b. The person may make a wrong prediction about the nature of his or her future values. ("I'll never learn to enjoy the kind of activities open to me now that I am confined to a wheelchair.")

c. The person may have mistaken values.

6. In judging whether a person would be better off dead, we must take into account not only the person's present and future values but also his or her personal ideals and personal integrity (Jeremy, for example).

Ω

The Survivor's Rights

Graber's logical analysis, Fletcher's argument on moral and ethical grounds, and Danto's and Weitzman's empirical data all indicate that suicide is and in some instances should be justified for humane reasons. Aside from some consideration by Graber, however, the issue of the rights of those whom the suicide leaves behind remains to be explored. Before granting that suicide may be justifiable at least in some instances, should we consider the rights of the suicide's survivors that they not be bereaved?

In the broadest sense, as members of the public, do we have a right that persons not commit suicide in our presence? Although such cases have not been studied, individuals have been severely traumatized by seeing another person kill himself or herself. Do people in public places, in train stations, or on sidewalks beside tall buildings have a right to be free of the grotesque spectacle of public suicide?

In terms of custodial relationships, do those—whether parents, physicians, or prison guards—entrusted with the lives of their wards have responsibilities transcending the rights of those for whom they care? If you see a stranger about to jump from a bridge, are your responsibilities any different than if the would-be suicide is your brother? your spouse? your patient? your ward? The answer most often given is that the relationship between the suicide and others must be considered in discussing the justifiability of the act.

Death is social, we argued at the outset, and now we can extend that argument to suicide. As one kind of death, suicide, too, results from relationships between people, between individuals and society. As one kind of death, suicide, too, ruptures relationships between people, between individuals and society. Analysis of suicide solely from the point of view of the individual is therefore incomplete. The larger context of interpersonal relationships and the consequences for society must also be considered.

In the early 1960s while living in Puerto Rico, Wallace studied the acts of interpersonal aggression, homicide, and aggravated assault, which are frequent in Latin cultures. Following a theme that was first introduced into the literature by Hans von Hentig (1940), he became interested in the way in which some victims precipitate their own demise. Assault takes place between two or more people, he argued (1962), within a social setting that structures subsequent events, including the outcome. Within this setting some people commit suicide by provoking others into murdering them. Drawing upon this background, Wallace begins the following essay by drawing some general parallels between suicide and homicide.

Is homicide justifiable? Wallace asks. The answer depends on what type of homicide we are asking about. Until we specify the type of homicide in question, no meaningful answer can be given. Is it a police officer killing an escaping convict or a sniper shooting into a crowd? As with homicide, Wallace argues that we must distinguish between types of suicide.

Once we recognize the well-established empirical variation in types of suicide, Wallace argues, some types will then be seen to be clearly not justifiable while others may be so considered. In the typology that he offers, Wallace also points out the parallels between some types of suicide and euthanasia.

Thus far we have talked only of suicide. With the following article, let us now conclude our examination of suicide, ending with the beginning of our discussion of euthanasia.

The Right to Live and the Right to Die

Samuel E. Wallace

Suicide and homicide have been related to each other in theory and research, but in social policy they have been treated as distinctly different events. Gold (1958) and Bohannon (1960), among others, have studied suicide and homicide as crimes. Freud (1933), Menninger (1938), and Dollard (1939) have seen both as having common origin in aggression. Verkko (1951) and Porterfield (1959; 1960) are among those who have examined their inverse relationship in frequency of occurrence, while Henry and Short (1954), Quinney (1965), and Gibbs and Martin (1964) have investigated the dual tie of suicide and homicide to the economic cycle. In spite of these established commonalities and interrelationships, social policy characteristically has specified incarceration for those who commit homicide, while therapy is suggested for those who would commit suicide.

Since the perpetrator and victim are, of course, one and the same in successful suicide, legal sanctions against the suicide are obviously impossible, and this also has led to different treatment of suicide and homicide. The inability of law to punish those guilty of the crime of suicide has led some to suggest suicide be decriminalized on the grounds that what the law is powerless to prevent it should not attempt to regulate (Silving, 1957). Believing that law regulates only the relationship between persons, Ferri (1925) argued that it was illogical for there to be a crime against oneself. Further, he argued that every person had a "right" to dispose of his or her own life.

The complexities of the issue and the inability of the law to punish the suicide have combined to relegate the legal punishment of suicide to a history of default, without having clarified a coherent course of social policy. As a result, wide policy variations have been accorded both suicide and those who attempt it. According to legal scholar Helen Silving, "World legislation on the subject of suicide is more widely split than on any other topic" (1957).

It is our thesis that death from any cause is a social event. As an instrument of social policy, law can no more legitimize any and all forms of death than it can any and all forms of life; death as well as life has profound consequences on the society and upon those individual persons who constitute it. Just as the actions of an individual while living, whether of negligence or malice aforethought, may have harmful consequences for another, so may an individual's actions in dying have harmful consequences. We agree with Silving (1957) that "the 'personality' rights of man include the right to dispose of his own life," but exceptions must be made when such actions cause harm to another, either intentionally or by criminal negligence. Human responsibility extends throughout life, through its last moment until death.

The law of homicide provides the most instructive example of dealing with death due to suicide, in part because both homicide and suicide involve killing. Through lengthy tradition, numerous statutes, and case law, homicide has been differentiated into justifiable killing as well as murder and manslaughter. There is widespread agreement on the types of homicide as well as on the identifying features of each type. For example, most jurisdictions agree that a police officer who shoots and kills an escaping convict is committing a justifiable homicide. The person who kills another with premeditation, intentionally, and with malice aforethought is said to have committed that act of unjustifiable homicide that we call murder in the first degree. Unjustifiable homicide also includes manslaughter, which like murder, is divided into first and second degree.

Homicide is thus commonly classified by law into a broad category by the resulting harm, that is, the death of another, and then within the category by the extent of the accompanying subjective participation in the act itself. Depending on the subjective participation, the act is termed first or second degree murder or voluntary or involuntary manslaughter (Mueller, 1958). Further, "whenever a circumstance of justification or excuse is partially present, malice aforethought is cancelled and voluntary manslaughter is the offense made out" (Wallace and Canals, 1962). The law points out the incompatibility between justification and malice aforethought, a principle whose importance will soon become evident.

As murder, manslaughter, and justifiable homicide are all classified together according to the harm produced, so are all acts of suicide grouped together. However, neither the law nor social policy differentiates suicide into its various types, even though a century of empirical research has thoroughly documented its distinct typological variations (Maris, 1969; Durkheim, 1951; Shneidman, 1967). Within the lay public, and all too often in professional circles as well, suicide is treated as if it were but a unitary act without variation. Whether suicide is condemned or justified, the arguments are as mistaken as they would be if applied to all homicide. Treating all suicides alike is rather like asking whether one can or cannot rightfully kill another while ignoring any difference between self-defense and wanton murder. Predictably, those who attempt to defend homicide have the duties of police officers in mind while those who condemn homicide are referring to malicious murders. Any possible area for agreement is rendered impossible by the initial failure to specify the type of homicide that is being discussed. The parallel to discussions of the defensibility of suicide is evident.

Clearly the essential first step in any discussion of suicide is to specify the types of suicide that authorities believe to exist. After the types of suicide have been established or at least generally accepted, meaningful dialogue about the relations between types of suicide and euthanasia, our present concern, may commence. Therefore a few of the many studies of suicide will be reviewed in order to document the nearly universal finding that there are distinctly different types of suicide, whatever they may be called.

Types of Suicide

Empirical research on suicide began over a century ago with Quetelet's 1835 publication. Since then nearly thirty-five hundred books and articles have been published on the subject (Caplow, 1973). In 1897 Durkheim (1951) identified egoistic, altruistic, and anomic suicide and added a fourth type, fatalistic suicide, for historical interest. Freud (1933) and his followers characteristically treated suicide as the manifestation of a single universal death instinct. Menninger (1938) differentiated the sources of this instinct into three types: (*a*) impulses derived from the primary aggressiveness crystallized as a wish to kill, (*b*) impulses derived from a modification of the primary aggressiveness crystallized as a wish to be killed, and (*c*) impulses from primary aggressiveness and additional sophisticated motives crystallized as the wish to die. Shneidman and Farberow (1957) posited four types of suicide—referred, surcease, cultural, and psychotic—and outlined distinctly different suggested modes of treatment for them. Concluding one of the many reviews of the literature available, Jackson (1957) stated, "These various emphases point up the idea that suicide is a symptomatic act, not a discrete entity."

The types of suicide do vary widely, and their differences do stem from important differences in theoretical explanation. While controversy with respect to any typology abounds, nearly all researchers agree that the category of suicide contains different types within it. Theories typically parallel an empirically observed differentiation. Whether suicide is conceived as a problem of religion (Eckhardt, 1973) or as an issue of law (Silving, 1954), such discussions also underscore the processes of social construction leading to the category of suicide and the different types of acts contained within it (Douglas, 1967).

A Proposed Typology

Since the identification of any specific typology will find less agreement than the need for typology of some kind, we offer the following types so as to promote the discussion of the relationship between types of suicide and the right to die. Although the types are described with cases drawn from the author's study of bereavement from suicide (Wallace, 1973), the typology itself was developed from a review of the literature. Three of the specific types are drawn in part from Menninger's *Man Against Himself* (1938) but are presented herein as separate types, whereas Menninger argues that these three wishes must be concurrently present for the death instinct to become manifest. Acceptance of Menninger's theoretical explanation is not implied.

In addition, the typology presented herein is based on extensions of the law on homicide to suicide. While there are obvious differences between suicide and homicide, especially in that the harm produced in the former is to the self while for the latter it is against another, even this difference falsely ignores the factual harm produced. Both suicide and homicide are to some extent willful, even if sometimes only through negligence (as in involuntary manslaughter). Both produce the harm of death. The fact that the harm of death is produced in the perpetrator, while removing the criminal from the jurisdiction of law, cannot be taken to mean that as an instrument of social policy the law would therefore be silent. Otherwise, by extension, we would have to say that there is no crime of murder when its perpetrator is found dead. Act and actor are separated, and a crime is said to have been committed whether or not the actor is or can be punished – in part because it is other such acts that the law seeks to prevent.

Pursued from yet another angle, murder is said to have occurred whether the specific person committing that act is known or unknown, alive or dead. Likewise the suicide, even though he may truly be said to have suffered already the maximum penalty that the state can impose (capital punishment), may or may not nevertheless be said to have committed a crime – because the existence of a criminal act does not rest upon the presence or absence of the person responsible. Suicide may thus be held to be a crime even though it is directed against the self and even though its perpetrator may be beyond the jurisdiction of the law.

Murder is punished only in part because of the specific harm produced. It is also punished to prevent future such acts, not only by a specific murderer, but also by others. The success or failure of that policy is not at issue. The point rather is that as an instrument of social policy, law seeks to regulate, influence, and sanction conduct. Although a person is already dead in the instance of an act of murder and the law cannot change that outcome, nevertheless the murderer is punished not only for his act but for the protection of others as well. The law seeks to protect others from the harmful acts in which some may engage. Punishment is not the sole, even if it is the principal, aim. Therefore, if the law decides that suicide is indeed a harm, it may prohibit suicide, even though the perpetrators cannot be punished, on the grounds that others may be persuaded not to suicide. Possibly even some of those who wish to die may not wish to do so if they become criminals by that act. Furthermore, a vigorous social policy that is supported by institutions other than the law, such as religious and civic organizations, may be presumed to have a potential deterrent effect.

It should be reiterated that thus far we have contended only that crimes consist of harms produced, that harms exist independent of the presence or absence of the perpetrator, and that as an instrument of social policy, law has objectives beyond that of punishing persons convicted of producing harms. Whether or not suicide constitutes a harm remains to be established.

Drawing upon our initial discussion, we should reintroduce here the importance of clearly specifying the types of acts included within the broad category of suicide, that is, all those acts resulting in death that are said to have been produced by the decedents' own actions.

Mislabeled Suicide

Contrary in this instance to homicide, medical authorities alone are responsible for identifying instances of suicide. Under most jurisdictions in the United States, cause of death is determined by an attending physician or, if a person dies without a physician in attendance, by a medical examiner. Because of the prevailing practice of relying upon the findings of a single person, mistakes are bound to occur. Some suicides are therefore mislabeled. Since we are considering the social policy implications of types of suicide, recognition of mislabeling is important for the protection of the decedent and his or her survivors. Two variations fall within the type of suicide we will call mislabeled: the distorted and the mistaken. Instances of each will be given from the author's own study.

The mislabeled suicide is rarely mentioned in the literature, perhaps in part because it calls into question the procedures by which death is labeled in the United States. Its existence stems from the fact that not only is suicide a social construct, but instances of it are identified by imperfect human agents who are given the responsibility of deciding the cause of death. While we do not doubt the fine work of many dedicated medical examiners who practice in the United States, nevertheless in more than a few instances the determination of cause of death seems to be subject to political and institutional pressure.

When death occurs in total institutions or other spheres of institutional responsibility, a finding of suicide makes the decedent responsible for his or her death and thus absolves the authorities. Total institutions are those that exercise nearly complete control over the lives of their inmate populations. Total institutions like the military, religious cloisters, mental hospitals, and prisons feed their populations what and when they want, house them where and with whom they decide, dress and undress them at will, and in other ways determine the circumstances of their lives. Because of this control over the lives of inmates, total institutions are held responsible for inmate deaths.

When death does occur in such settings, the consequences for an institution are least when suicide is established as the cause because that determination makes the decedent rather than the authorities responsible. This is not to say that there are no consequences for the institution when suicide is found to have occurred, only that the consequences are less severe.

A finding of murder, for example, necessarily requires a search for a murderer – often a difficult procedure, especially in prisons. A finding of accidental death makes the authorities possibly guilty of negligence. To label a death as suicide avoids these difficulties for an institution and its responsible authorities. While it is true that often there is compelling evidence of the cause of death and thus no possible distortion, in less clearcut cases institutional pressures for a finding of suicide may be presumed to exist. In other words, when doubt exists, a determination of suicide is most likely.

Two such doubtful or borderline cases exist within the twelve originally studied by the author. Twenty-one-year-old Mr. Ago, after three months' incarceration of an expected term of fifteen months, on the day before he was to be transferred to a prison of his choice where he could learn his chosen trade, was found dead in his cell. Although his death was ruled a suicide by the prison physician, Mr. Ago's five-year heroin addiction, in addition to evidence of the availability of such drugs within that prison, suggests that he may have died from an overdose. For unknown reasons the authorities persuaded Mrs. Ago neither to view the body nor to have an autopsy performed. Obviously a finding that death was caused by an overdose of narcotics would have created severe problems for the administration of the prison. Suicide was a much more acceptable label.

The second instance of what we are calling distorted suicide was Mr. Banks, who was hit by a subway train. He was an alcoholic, recently separated from his wife, long unemployed and now destitute, and he was undeniably walking the surface train tracks at 1:30 A.M. Since there is no train service in Boston after midnight, it is difficult to argue that he would have expected a train. He might have been walking the tracks to his destination, as he had done before. "He did crazy things when he was drunk," his wife told us. A lawsuit against the transit authority might have resulted, and possibly for such a reason the politically appointed medical examiner ruled the death to be suicide. Some explanation would seem to be necessary for why the medical examiner wrote on the death certificate "death by suicide while walking tracks in state of deep depression" since the only evidence he had was the corpse. There were no witnesses, and no testimony was ever solicited from wife, children, or any of the man's friends or associates.

Suicide is a social construct, and the individual instances of it are identified by imperfect human agents. Recognizing this and understanding the circumstances under which deaths are so labeled are essential preliminary steps before either defending what we call suicide or linking it in any way to euthanasia.

Mistaken suicide also occurs. This type differs from what we have called distorted suicide in that the label affixed to the death makes a difference only to the survivors. Mistaken suicide refers to those on which the examiner may have simply made a mistake. In Massachusetts, where the author's study was conducted, medical examiners are political appointees and are paid a fee per case investigated. Although state law requires an autopsy for every case that comes under a medical examiner's jurisdiction and pays a separate fee for each one, in practice few autopsies are performed. Most examiners apparently feel that the small additional fee is not worth it. Under these circumstances, mistakes undoubtedly occur more often than need be.

In the most obvious of the two instances of this type of suicide, Mr. Tibbetts was found by his son at noon, face down on the kitchen floor, having died while making a cup of coffee. Forty-nine years old, living with his second wife and four sons, Mr. Tibbetts had returned with his wife late the previous night from a veterans' convention where he had managed to continue his three-year abstinence from alcohol. Mr. Tibbetts also had tuberculosis and had suffered from a nervous disorder since his forty-two months' incarceration in a Japanese POW camp. These various health problems had combined to require his retirement for medical reasons from the state civil service six months before his death. Although a neighboring physician initially ruled his death to be from coronary, the medical examiner ruled it to be suicide when he found barbiturates in a blood sample; he did not know that Mr. Tibbetts had been regularly taking sedatives for some twenty years.

Other relevant data like Mr. Tibbetts' forty-five-pound weight loss in the preceding six months suggest that possibly the medical examiner was simply incorrect in his diagnosis. Since his finding was not released until two weeks after burial, the autopsy that the medical examiner should have initially performed was by then no longer possible. In this instance, as in the second in which a non-medically controlled epileptic was ruled to have committed suicide by drowning in the bathtub, incompetent and unconcerned physicians may have simply made a mistake. In any kind of work, mistakes do happen. Their relevance to our study lies in excluding them from the acts of suicide relevant to a discussion of euthanasia. The issue is of more than academic interest since research findings are characteristically based on all cases labeled suicide by the medical examiner.

The social policy implications of both distorted and mistaken suicide lie in the direction of improving the process by which death, especially suicide, is labeled. Under current law in Massachusetts and in operation in many other states as well, the attending physician alone or, when death occurs without a physician in attendance, the medical examiner (sometimes called a coroner) alone makes that important determination. Survivors are typically without any right to testify or to submit other evidence. If the decedent's survivors wish to challenge the physician's determination, they must do so in open court, making public intimate details of the lives of the dead as well as the living.

The low pay, the doubtful reputation, the marginal medical competence of too many medical examiners stand as mute testimony to our death-denying culture and to the inadequate importance we give to death-related matters. A change in social policy is long overdue.

An important right that is involved in these two variations of mislabeled suicide is significantly related to the right to die. This is the right to an accurate determination of cause of death, one fully supported by evidence. Whatever the right to die may be, until and unless cause of death is accurately determined, people will continue to die from whatever physicians decide they have died from, be they trusted family physicians or unknown political appointees. Is not the granting of this right in theory as well as in practice the essential first step involved in any right to die?

Since the finding of death by suicide is in fact a social psychiatric as well as a medical decision (Shneidman and Farberow, 1957), one beyond the training of many medical examiners, we propose that for a finding of suicide the concurring opinion of a psychiatrist be required, that survivors be legally entitled to submit any data they consider relevant, and that a special report, perhaps a psychological autopsy, also be required. Since suicide has such severe emotional, social, and for some, religious and economic consequences, changes in the process of determining cause of death should begin with suicide, but everyone should have an accurate determination of cause of death.

Nonjustifiable Suicide

In most deaths that are labeled as suicides, unmistakable evidence usually exists that documents without question that suicide occurred. It remains to classify those acts that are correctly labeled by the types of suicide they represent. Continuing to use the law of homicide as our guide in formulating social policy directives, we will contend that types of suicide should be established on the basis of the harm produced. The fact that harm is produced by at least some types of suicide is abundantly clear from a wide variety of sources.

"The person who commits suicide puts his psychological skeleton in the survivors' emotional closet—he sentences the survivor to a complex of negative feelings and, most importantly, to obsessing about the reasons for the suicide death" (Shneidman, 1967).

The reality of this statement is seen in the remarks of the widows bereaved by suicide whom the author (1973) interviewed. "Well, I'm very anti men. . . . I feel I've been used and I can never really love somebody for himself. . . . As far as sex is concerned – I just – I don't think I'm ever going to be able to feel that way about a man again." "I don't think I'd care if I never remarried again – I'd rather stay single. . . . I don't think that I'm that great a wife that I want to – you know – ruin somebody else's life."

Rather than permit his wife to leave him, twenty-year-old Mr. Jefferson hanged himself in the bathroom, leaving a note on the front door for his wife saying, "Cathy I love you. You're right, I am crazy . . . and thank you for trying to love me. Phil." Mrs. Jefferson felt and frequently insisted that she "killed Phil." She attempted suicide herself a week after Phil's death.

Further details are not necessary here because this type of suicide and the harm it produces are well recognized in the literature. Following Freud, Menninger argues that this type of suicide springs from the desire to kill. Although the self is the obvious victim in all suicides, the intention of some is the wish to harm, hurt, or destroy another. "Murder in one hundred and eighty degrees" it is sometimes called, the symbolic murder of another.

Murderous suicide we would label this type of suicide because it is committed with malice aforethought. It communicates to another, especially one's spouse, "You did this to me." That this message is received is evident in the guilt, the obsessional search for an explanation, the suicidal behavior, and the morbid grief reactions that this type of suicide characteristically provokes.

Persons who harbor a hate so overpowering as to kill themselves in order to hurt and harm others cannot be said to be truly alive. The deep and fundamental joy of living is absent from the murderous suicide. Hate makes this act of suicide truly blind, for in infantile fashion, murderous suicides do not see the fact that they will not be around to witness the hurt they are so intent on causing. Social policy should be directed toward the survivors who have suffered from such an attack on their own lives. They should be extended full medical and psychiatric support to help them survive in a healthful way.

The question of the survivor's responsibility for the hate of the suicide is sometimes raised (Kobler, 1964; Jourard, 1969). In our study, while only one widow stated that someone had actually told her that she "drove him to it," most widows said they felt that some people thought they had been "to blame." No matter how a person may have been contributory, surely no one may be held responsible for another's suicide. When and if the survivor is considered to have been responsible, in that same measure the survivor's already weighty burden is increased, while needed social support is withdrawn. A changed societal reaction is thus needed with respect to this type of suicide, a reaction that does not make such suicide legitimate or give anyone the right to die under such circumstances but that does support the living. To consider as legitimate, acceptable, or defensible in any way the suicide that is murderous in intent furthermore cannot be considered to involve the suicide's right to live because another life is endangered. To fail to censure such acts would imply acceptance of murder in one hundred and eighty degrees.

It may be contended that categorizing acts by the actor's intention is not possible since the responses of others may differ from what the actor intended. Indeed, even within the cases being reviewed here, there are widows who saw murderous intent where there probably was none. The identification of specific cases falling within the type offered, however, is an empirical matter. The evidence for the existence of the type of suicide called murderous is clear. Which specific instances should be so labeled depends on rules of evidence and documentation; the existence of the type remains.

Murderous suicide is one of the three types of nonjustifiable suicide. The harm it produces is the most severe. In part, the malice with which it is done makes it nonjustifiable, and in part it is nonjustifiable because of the factual harm produced. This does not mean that the suicide should be punished or that the survivors should suffer at the hands of the state, but rather that the public should recognize malice in cases of this type and should endeavor to help the survivors live through this life-threatening attack. Prevention of this type of suicide should meanwhile be pursued with all possible vigor.

Criminal homicide is divided into murder and manslaughter largely on the basis of malice aforethought, and types of suicide also can be profitably distinguished in these terms. Like homicide, suicide can be further distinguished into voluntary and involuntary types. Voluntary manslaughter in homicide roughly corresponds to that type of suicide that Menninger argues is the manifestation of the wish to be killed. The label we tentatively affix to this type of suicide is *masochistic*. Having conducted their own trials and found themselves guilty, these persons seem to proceed to carry out their own self-imposed sentences.

In the cases discussed in this paper, Mr. Grenon may be seen as illustrative. Married for twenty-seven years, having two children who were in their twenties at the time of his death, Mr. Grenon had been a successful business executive until the onset of the severe phases of his alcoholism. Separated from his wife and family, having become loathsome in his own eyes, he may be said to have wished to be killed for all the hurt he had caused those closest to him. He felt both guilty and worthless.

Early treatment and effective rehabilitation are needed for a person prone to this type of suicide, not arguments for the person's right to die. The implications for social policy are that enhanced social services and programs designed to rescue and rebuild human potential are needed to help those who would take their lives because they feel they are worthless or are less than human.

Euthanasia traditionally means a quiet and easy death or the means or the act of procuring it. Neither the murderous nor the masochistic suicide can be held to fall within the realm of euthanasia. Nor should any society forfeit its responsibility to its members by considering that they have the right to die under such circumstances. Rather the society must redouble its efforts to provide everyone with a significant life, for both of these types of suicide document societal failure to provide meaning in life.

Involuntary manslaughter also has its parallel in suicide, which we shall call, again for the purposes of discussion, *suicide by surrender*. The critical element in this type of suicide is that the person, rightly or wrongly, feels that the decision about whether to live is not that person's decision to make. Whereas the murderous suicide has the freedom to live and has decided to die and the masochist feels that life is not worth living but is free to choose, the suicide by surrender gives to others the decision for life or death. In this type of suicide, the person surrenders the decision about his or her life and death to others.

Often with much forewarning, through certain behavior, this would-be suicide says that what happens is up to others believed to control his or her fate. In this type of suicide the person feels a lack of control over either life or death. Since total institutions in effect assume responsibility for the total life of their inmates, we may expect this type of suicide to occur within them. The single instance in the twelve cases originally studied, however, took place outside a total institution, in a small apartment house.

After eighteen years of marriage, the last ten of which were spent supporting her alcoholic, physically abusive, and work-disabled husband, Mrs. Miller by court order had her husband placed in a state mental hospital. His friends secured his release to their custody somewhat later, and he rented an apartment on the first floor of the three-story apartment building where his wife and five children lived. Prevented then by court order from bothering his family and unsuccessful in getting any response to the many reportedly obscene and threatening notes he posted in the stairwell and on their door, he then made it their decision about whether he would live or die.

An hour before church was to be over one Sunday, Mr. Miller placed some ten or twelve notes throughout the apartment house, saying, among other things, that he hoped his family would take him back if he came "through this." Then with all the windows and the door of his apartment open, he began to take an assortment of pills, writing down the number and type of each. The family ignored the notes, his open door, and the sight of Mr. Miller slumped over the kitchen table when they came home from church ("He's probably just drunk again"), and it was not until a neighbor investigated in the late afternoon that he was taken, too late, to the hospital.

Whether what we have called suicide by surrender takes place within or outside a total institution makes no difference as far as the right to die is concerned. The clear implication of this type of suicide for social policy is that all possible means should be used to prevent its occurrence. Total institutions are an abomination in the first place. No one should be forced to live or to die under such circumstances of total life and death control. When inmates engage in actions that indicate that they feel they have no control over their own lives or deaths, they are reflecting what is all too often the existential reality of total institutions like prisons. The response in terms of social policy should be to change the nature of such institutions, to see in such suicide the compelling need for their reform. Neither individual nor institution is well served by accepting such circumstances of death.

However difficult it may be to reform the nature of total institutions, it is even more difficult to prevent suicides by surrender that occur outside total institutions. Mr. Miller had been in contact with several programs and agencies of rehabilitation to no avail. Whatever the solution, this type of suicide cannot be held to involve any right to die. On the contrary, these persons had a right to live, a right that was abrogated by society as they found it.

It is not being contended that suicide or specific types of suicide be treated as crimes. Rather, discussions concerning the right to live and the right to die ought to take into account the harm produced by suicides, and social policy should be developed accordingly.

Justifiable Suicide

We have considered three types of nonjustifiable suicide, all of which produce grave harm to suicides and their survivors. We now can discuss the final category of justifiable suicide. In contrast to the nonjustifiable suicide, this type of suicide cannot be held to produce such grave harm. This person wishes to die and has characteristically put his or her affairs in order. The survivors have been cared for; even goodbyes have often been said, although not always acknowledged.

All suicide, being a willful action, leaves things in a particular state. The nature of the decedent's affairs is thus the most reliable clue to the type of suicide that has been committed. Grief reactions are another set of data to consider. In all there is the pain of loss, the absence of a relationship. When survivors feel the death to be justifiable under the circumstances, however, the suffering occasioned by the loss is easier to accept.

Suicide that we can accept, justify, and argue for social policy to allow seems to fall into two types of life circumstances: those involving persons who wish to die and can procure the means for their death and those involving persons who cannot. The latter include the terminally ill without reasonable hope of recovery who are in pain and wish for surcease. These victims have been thoroughly discussed in the literature and should be placed in the category of justifiable suicide.

Those outside a medical facility who are also in pain and equally in search of surcease should also be related to euthanasia. Consider the person called Mr. Sullivan in the research to which we have been referring. Married for thirty-two years, during which he helped to rear his five children, Mr. Sullivan throughout his life was hard-working, responsible, religious, involved, and, in general, admirable. At age thirty-eight he had been seriously injured at work, and the resulting paralysis below the waist thereafter confined him to a wheelchair. After five or six unsuccessful operations over many years following his accident, he vowed never again to consult a doctor or go to a hospital, and he never did. Twenty-four years after his accident, his youngest graduated from high school and Mr. Sullivan's health began to deteriorate.

During the last few months of his life, Mr. Sullivan stayed up late at night to go through all his belongings, even the letters he had written to his wife while he was in World War II. Late one night he quietly left the house, drove his specially equipped car to a bridge, and although on crutches, he managed to climb over the rail to fall into the river below.

When his suicide is contrasted with any of the others described earlier, the differences between the types of suicide are underscored, and the justifiability of this type of suicide is evident. Although Mrs. Sullivan understood her husband's actions in a way, her religious orientation, her family, friends, and community made it difficult for her to accept the "crime" that her husband had committed, for no one recognized differences in types of suicide.

Justifiable suicide, like justifiable homicide, does exist. To recognize it requires that we differentiate the broad socially constructed category of suicide into its various distinct types. Discussion of the relationship between suicide and euthanasia must therefore begin at the point where the accumulated empirical findings have taken us, namely, with the recognition of different types of suicides. It is our thesis that only the type of suicide that stems from the wish to die under circumstances of concern for the suicide's survivors can be legitimately related to euthanasia. Such conditions may stem from cultural sources, as in the loss of honor; they may originate in the desire for the surcease from pain. Recognizing that the wish to die and the context that honors that wish may spring from several sources, we can link only this type of suicide to euthanasia.

Labeling death natural, accidental, suicidal, or homicidal obscures the intention of the person vis-à-vis his or her own death. Some just wish to die, others wish to be rid of the pain of living, and others wish to kill or harm another. Death cannot become humanized until each person's individual death is recognized.

Consider the matter from the point of view of the person who is dying. The person wishes to die in order to be released from the enduring pain of a life without a future. If this individual has the means, suicide will be committed. Without the means to do so, as would be true if the individual is hospitalized, an individual cannot commit suicide even though the intention remains the same.

Justifiable suicide and voluntary euthanasia thus become joined from the perspective of the person whose death it is. The two become separated only by the externalities of whether the person has the means — the poison, the overdose, the pistol, the bridge. Deprived of virtually all freedom to act in total institutions such as our hospitals, the dying sink deeper into depression as they hear their caretakers say, "And we do it all for you."

Conclusion

The right to die must include the right to an accurate determination of cause of death, and thus our first type of suicide, the mislabeled, must end. Whether it is distorted or mistaken, done willfully or through negligence, to label as suicide that which is not creates unnecessary suffering. Since the label of suicide has such severe emotional, social, and, for some people, religious and economic consequences, special supporting data for such a finding should be required, perhaps a psychological autopsy.

Suicide must be recognized to constitute as broad a category as homicide does, containing within it distinctly different types. Thirty-five hundred research reports published over a 140-year period have definitely established that there are different types of suicide. In this article we first identified three types of nonjustifiable suicide—murderous, masochistic, and suicide by surrender—and recommended social policy changes for each type.

The fourth and final type of suicide that we identified was called justifiable. It was pointed out that the difference between justifiable suicide and voluntary euthanasia lay in whether an individual had the means to carry out a desire for suicide. Depriving individuals of their freedom may ensure their survival, but it becomes difficult to see how such policy enhances the value of life.

The right to live entails at least some measure of freedom to choose how we wish to live, at least in democracies. To be told how to live, where and with whom, and to be without control over the other aspects of our lives such as when to sleep and when to wake, what to eat, when, and with whom to talk—to be deprived of the choice of how to live in the name of the sanctity of life—would surely seem like some cruel hoax. Yet it seems that this is in fact what we do with the dying. Through measures such as institutionalization we deprive them of their freedom. Being unfree, they can neither live nor die. And thus, some argue, the sanctity of life is upheld.

Ω

Euthanasia As Assisted Suicide

With the Wallace article the relationship between suicide and euthanasia becomes clear: euthanasia is assisted suicide. Fletcher states that the relationship between suicide and euthanasia is so close that "to justify either one . . . is to justify the other."

Before addressing the issues of euthanasia, however, we need to recognize that there are alternatives other than dying in pain or begging to be killed. As Twycross points out in the following selection, control of pain is now more possible than ever before. Therefore for physicians to fail to administer pain-relieving medications is often inappropriate treatment.

Earlier we noted that some persons commit suicide because the "pain" of life is too great. We argued that they need improved social conditions and enhanced social well-being, not justifications for their suicide. In parallel fashion Twycross documents cases in which persons may say that they prefer death rather than to continue the endless pain they have suffered. Twycross forcibly argues that such persons need proper medical relief of pain, not euthanasia. For the doctor to prolong the distress of the dying patient is not, in his view, legal, moral, or ethical.

Voluntary Euthanasia*

Robert G. Twycross

The two extremes of dying in pain and being killed do not exhaust the possibilities for the stricken patient. (Horder, 1936)

Forty years ago in Britain, the Voluntary Euthanasia Society was founded. Its aim was "to create a public opinion favorable to the view that an adult person suffering from a fatal illness, for which no cure is known, should be entitled by law to the mercy of a painless death if and when that is his expressed wish: and to promote this legislation." The society was formed by Dr. Killick Millard as a result of enthusiasm engendered by his presidential address to the Society of Medical Officers of Health in 1931. Dr. Millard (1931) asserted that "vast numbers of human beings are doomed to end their earthly existence by a lingering, painful, and often agonising form of death. Voluntary euthanasia should be legalized for adults suffering from an incurable, fatal, painful disease."

Since then, two bills aimed at legalizing voluntary euthanasia have been presented to Parliament – in 1936 and 1969. Although defeated, they stimulated discussion of the issues involved, and as a result, euthanasia has come to mean the legalized killing of a person –

1. who is suffering form an incurable, distressing physical condition;
2. who is over the age of eighteen;
3. who is in his right mind;
4. who personally and voluntarily requests that such a procedure be carried out.

Until recently, much of the debate has been centered on death from cancer. Accordingly, we will deal predominantly with this aspect. Further, although cancer patients may experience a wide variety of distressing symptoms, discussion has been confined largely to the question of pain control. For the sake of brevity we will do likewise.

*Translated by the editors from "Freiwillige Euthanasie – Eine klinische Betrachtung," initially published in *Suizid und Euthanasie*, ed. Albin Eser (Stuttgart: Enke, 1976).

The Nature of Pain

To most people, pain and incurable cancer appear inextricably intertwined. Such an opinion was given encouragement by the National Society for Cancer Relief when it appealed for funds following the death of the young British athlete Lilian Board in 1972. A poster, subsequently withdrawn on account of criticism, stated that:

> Lilian's death proved how cruel cancer can be
> Cancer chills the body
> Fierce pain is often its hallmark

In fact, published data suggest that as many as 50 percent of all terminal cancer patients have no pain at all or minimal discomfort at most (Turnbull, 1954). Forty percent do, however, experience severe pain, and the remaining 10 percent suffer pain of a less intense nature (Aitken-Swan, 1959).

Pain associated with advanced cancer is usually chronic, constant in nature even if variable in intensity. Unfortunately for a patient, the physician's understanding of pain is taken from personal experience of acute pain—the toothache, the headache, the cut or bruise—all of which tend to pass quite quickly. On the other hand, chronic pain is a situation rather than an event, and it—

1. is impossible to predict when it will end;
2. usually gets worse rather than better;
3. appears to be meaningless;
4. frequently expands to occupy the patient's whole attention, isolating him from the world around.

Pain should, therefore, be regarded not simply as a sensation but as a dual phenomenon, one part being the perception of the sensation and the other the patient's emotional reaction to it. Depression, anxiety, fear, other unrelieved symptoms, and pain itself all tend to exacerbate the total pain experience.

At a weekly seminar for interns in general medicine (British Medical Journal 2:704–5) patients encountered in routine work were discussed in order to demonstrate that psychological factors can exist even in an apparently straightforward physical illness. On one occasion, discussion centered on the problem of a patient who had metastases in bone from disseminated breast cancer and whose pain remained unrelieved by narcotic analgesics. During the seminar it was suggested that the woman might be angry that neither her doctors nor her relatives would admit to her that she was dying and discuss the problems created by the situation and that she was expressing her anger in her complaints of pain. In fact, this proved to be the right explanation, and a full and frank discussion with the patient caused a dramatic improvement in her mental state, and she no longer complained of pain.

A diagnosis of cancer does not necessarily mean that the malignant process is responsible for the patient's pain. As always, diagnosis must precede treatment. Constipation, peptic ulcer, bedsores, cystitis, or musculoskeletal pains may prove to be the cause of pain and demand specific treatment.

Pain Control

Patients in pain require analgesia; nonnarcotic analgesics should be tried initially. The right dose of any analgesic is the one that gives adequate relief for a reasonable period of time. Patients do not want to be constantly taking tablets or receiving injections. A four-hour interval between doses should be regarded as the norm, although, on occasion, a shorter period may be necessary.

"Four hourly as necessary" has little or no place in the treatment of cancer pain. Chronic pain, whatever the etiology, requires regular preventive therapy. The aim is to titrate the level of analgesia against the patient's pain, gradually increasing the dose until the patient is pain-free, the next dose being given before the effect of the previous one has worn off and therefore before the patient may think it necessary. It is thus possible to erase the memory and fear of pain.

Once a drug has been shown to be ineffective, the patient should be transferred to a stronger alternative. This, in many cases, will need to be a narcotic analgesic. As nausea and vomiting are commonly associated with use of narcotics, especially in patients with advanced cancer, an anti-emetic should be given concurrently. If, to maintain an adequate level of analgesia, the dose has to be increased considerably over a short period of time, the patient may at first feel sleepy, but tolerance to the sedative effect generally occurs within two or three days.

Cancer can cause pain in many parts of the body. The pain of a metastasis in bone may be eased by the correct use of analgesics, but radiotherapy should be considered in such cases. Headache due to intracranial pressure is best treated with a glucocorticosteroid with or without an analgesic. Pain such as that caused by involvement of the brachial plexus or sciatic nerve may be best treated by tractotomy or phenol nerve block. In practice, a variety of measures may be used concurrently. In this connection the value of diversional activity should not be forgotten. Such activities can range from backrubs to occupational therapy, talking books, radio and television shows, conversation with others, and dayroom activities. Pain feels worse when it occupies the entire life field. Diversional activity does much more than just "pass the time"; it also diminishes the pain. Both attention and consciousness are essential to the perception of pain. The patient can reduce one or the other, but the reduction of attention can often be surprisingly effective.

Narcotic Analgesics in Perspective

Attention has been drawn (Marks and Sachar, 1973) to a form of iatrogenic drug abuse—the failure to treat patients in severe pain with adequate doses of narcotic analgesics (a matter of too little being given too late or not at all). It appears that, because of fears of addiction, rapid escalation of dose, and impairment of mental faculties, doctors generally are reluctant to prescribe narcotic analgesics even for patients who have advanced cancer. In order for the incidence and severity of these complications to be assessed, it was decided to review a series of 500 patients with terminal cancer who were admitted to St. Christopher's Hospice, London, where diamorphine (heroin) is the strong analgesic of choice (Twycross, 1974).

More than 80 percent of the patients received diamorphine, usually for severe pain and occasionally for distressing cough or dyspnea due to the malignant process or for general discomfort when other measures had failed. Fifteen percent of the patients received diamorphine either predominately or entirely by injection, the rest by mouth in an elixir containing both diamorphine and cocaine. The analgesic was administered regularly every four hours in order to achieve and maintain pain relief. The initial dose of diamorphine varied between 2.5–10 mg by mouth and was adjusted until effective analgesia was obtained. More than 60 percent of the patients were maintained on a dose of 10 mg or less, and only 8 percent required more than 30 mg. The dose of cocaine remained unchanged at 10 mg. With the aid of a night sedative, many patients did not require a dose in the middle of the night, but if necessary the patient was wakened for further medication and not left to wake up later in pain. Ultimately, most patients were transferred to parenterally administered diamorphine for the last twelve to twenty-four hours on account of increasing debility.

Dose-time graphs prepared for the 108 patients who received diamorphine for at least four weeks indicated that there were four general patterns of diamorphine requirement. These were categorized as—

1. step-plateau-step-plateau;
2. plateau;
3. undulating;
4. crescendo-diminuendo.

Their incidence was approximately 40, 40, 15, and 5 percent respectively. It was concluded that—

1. although most patients receive parenteral diamorphine during the last twelve to twenty-four hours, the majority can be maintained on oral medication prior to this time;
2. there is no single optimal dose of diamorphine;
3. psychological dependence does not occur;
4. physical dependence may develop but does not prevent the downward adjustment of the dose of diamorphine when considered clinically feasible;
5. the rate of dose increase becomes progressively less the longer the duration of treatment;
6. the prescription of diamorphine does not, by itself, lead to impairment of mental faculties.

Forty-six of the 500 patients were discharged for varying

lengths of time (days out and weekends not included), and of these, twenty-two were receiving diamorphine when discharged. They were all alert and mobile, although one or two of the more elderly used a walking frame. One of the patients wrote:

> How can I thank you all? To look back on those dreadful months of continuous sickness and pain that I endured at home, all the doctors' efforts seemed to have failed and things were indeed hopeless. The memory of coming to St. Christopher's, a helpless log, with no flexibility in my body and the pain that the slightest movement, or anyone's touch, caused me. It was like a miracle to me, the relief I felt, free from pain the first week and the gradual cure of the sickness and at last eating the first time for weeks. Now I go home walking again. Indeed, I am truly thankful.

A Case History

The following case history illustrates a number of the points highlighted in the review. Mr. H.B., a widowed street vendor aged sixty-nine, was admitted to St. Joseph's Hospice in May 1971. Cancer of the tongue had been diagnosed some three years earlier and had been treated by radium insertion. The following year he complained of pain in the floor of the mouth; this was relieved by nerve block. Fifteen months later a metastasis in the neck was treated with both radium and deep-radiation therapy. The pain subsequently returned but was controlled by oral pethidine (merperdine). After six months this proved inadequate, and the pain was not relieved despite the use of 10-mg morphine tablets every six hours. The radiotherapist wrote, "I have known this patient for two years and have previously been able to obtain adequate pain control, but can do so no longer."

When admitted, the patient complained of severe pain in the left side of the neck and a burning sensation in the mouth whenever he ate or drank. The constant pain made him sullen and apathetic, and he spent most of the day sitting by his bed fully clothed but doing nothing. In addition to local treatment, diamorphine, chlorpromazine, and an antibiotic were prescribed. The dose of diamorphine was increased, and after one week the chlorpromazine was replaced by another phenothiazine (methotrimeprazine). After two weeks the pain was fully relieved, and some ten days later he was discharged to his daughter's home.

For the next four months he was fully mobile and busied himself about the house and in the neighborhood. He then began to feel unwell and retired to bed. His daughter looked after him with the help of a district nurse until he died peacefully some days later. The dose of diamorphine remained unaltered throughout the outpatient period.

Inappropriate Treatment

There is little doubt that doctors and nurses often add to a patient's suffering by giving inappropriate treatment. Stomach tubes, drip-feeds, antibiotics, respirators, and cardiac resuscitation are all supportive measures for use in acute or subacute illnesses to assist a patient through a critical period toward recovery of health. Normally, to use such measures in the terminally ill, with no expectancy of a return to health, is bad medicine. A doctor has a duty to sustain life; a doctor has no duty—legal, moral, or ethical—to prolong the distress of a dying patient.

A doctor was asked in a coroner's court what treatment had been given to a patient with advanced cancer whose autopsy revealed fulminating pneumonia. The doctor replied that morphine had been used to quiet the cough and atropine used to help dry up the secretions. Nothing more was said by either doctor or coroner. There was no need, for in this situation the treatment was correct. Antibiotics would have been inappropriate. Pneumonia should still be the old man's and the dying cancer patient's friend. Yet many do not see it in terms of appropriate and inappropriate treatment but rather as a question, "to treat or not to treat?" This is quickly magnified into an ethical dilemma, and in the ensuing confusion, the patient suffers.

"Meddlesome medicine" is not always wholly the fault of the medical personnel involved. Sometimes doctors are actively encouraged to prescribe inappropriate treatment by relatives unwilling to face the inevitable. A man of seventy-five had a total laryngectomy for cancer of the larynx unresponsive to radiotherapy. Healing after operation was slow, and a fistula developed. His condition deteriorated, and a recurrence was noted in the posterior wall of the wound. Treatment with a cytotoxic preparation was unsuccessful, and he was subsequently admitted to the hospital because of increasing dysphagia. At the son's insistence and contrary to the doctor's recommendations, the patient was transferred to another hospital to have a feeding gastrostomy. Subsequently he was fed four times an hour. The patient was noted to be agitated at times and tended to be irritable when fed. He slowly deteriorated, having periods of drowsiness and fecal incontinence. Two months after the operation a nurse wrote, "For the past couple of weeks the patient has been trying to say something. Today when I went to give the 2 P.M. feed, he said quite clearly, with a look of panic and desperation on his face, 'Please, no more feeds.' He was waving his hand and holding on to me. Previously he had upset feeds deliberately. I talked to him, but he begged me not to feed him. I asked him if he wanted to die; he nodded and his expression changed to one of peaceful resignation. I gave him the feed; he half-heartedly tried to stop me, but he had become weak with all the agitation." After a few days, feeding was discontinued and the patient died peacefully five days later.

The Family

During a terminal illness the patient's relatives experience a variety of emotions. These will vary according to the depth of relationship between the patient and his family as well as by the duration of the illness and the mode of death. The following letter illustrates the family's need for support:

> What I thought were going to be bleak, desperately despairing, death-haunted weeks came to be one of the most life-enhancing experiences I have known. When you agreed to see me on that wet Saturday morning in September, I was in despair. I have had to cope with many things and can usually see something to do in most situations but I knew that, whatever I did, I would not be able to care for my mother in the way she needed. I have never felt so totally inadequate. When you intimated that you would be able to help, I did take heart a little; when you said there would be some happy days and happy memories to come, I found it hard to believe.
>
> So we arrived, and as she responded to the drugs, there

were such times, many more than I could have hoped for but . . . all too soon she gradually sank back into being unable to move, unable to communicate. It was a terrible emotional dilemma; I found myself so hoping it would soon be over yet so elated at any tiny response, clinging on while any sign of life remained. Mercifully – I think I can say that now – it didn't go on for long.

It was the most difficult time I have known, but I soon realized that I would not have to face it alone. I knew that, both physically and psychologically, everything was being done for my mother's comfort. I knew that she was with experienced and good people who did things for her that I would not have realized could be done. Though possessed of a sickening feeling of uselessness, I looked forward to visiting St. Christopher's each night. I never knew that there could be such nursing. That it should be consistently so was more than I could have dreamed of.

About four years ago a thirty-nine-year-old police sergeant with motor neurone disease was admitted to the hospice. He was an inpatient for about two years and from time to time discussed his attitude toward illness with one of the doctors. He disliked phrases such as "terminal" or "catastrophic illness"; instead, he preferred "bringing-together illness." When asked if he often saw this "bringing-together" happen, he replied, "Yes, I am a trained observer and I've been here for eighteen months. Patient and family, patient and staff, patient and patient – yes, it does happen" (Saunders, 1973:30–31). Terminal illness should not be regarded as an intrusion into life; it is part of life and can be a positive experience – a time of increasing maturity and deepening relationships.

Requests for Euthanasia

Patients rarely ask for euthanasia. Less rare is the patient who talks of suicide. A retired railway porter aged sixty-eight became increasingly unwell as a result of recurrent lung cancer. He began to abuse his relatives, withdrew from social contacts, and repeatedly threatened suicide. When admitted in April 1972, he was dirty, unkempt, and for the previous six weeks had been virtually bedfast due to marked weakness. He complained of widespread pain involving the chest, arms, and thighs. He was anorexic and constipated. It seemed likely that his symptoms were related to hypercalcaemia induced by the malignant process, and so he was given prednisone, together with an antidepressant. On this regime he steadily improved. He was symptom free and fully mobile within two weeks. Yet when he was admitted he had said he would like to put his head into a gas chamber. This was understandable in view of his condition – alone and virtually bedfast for six weeks. A week later, though washed and shaved and symptomatically improved, he still wanted to kill himself. After a further week he was asked again if he still wanted to gas himself. He replied, "I don't want to go home." It then came out that he was living in an apartment at the top of his son's house and the relationship between them was more than strained. On no account did he wish to go back there. He was relieved when assured that he was not expected to do so. For the rest of his time with us, he was fully active and enjoyed life in the hospital. He definitely no longer wished to die. A month after admission he suddenly became confused and had to be helped back to bed. He died an hour later.

More recently a patient who had a brain tumor made a number of remarks that suggested he wanted euthanasia, such as, "If I had a dog I'd put him down." When challenged to explain what he meant, he said, "You know what I mean." "Yes, I know what you mean. You are talking about euthanasia. Do you want it now?" "Oh no, not me" replied the patient. "I was thinking about some of the other patients!" A request for euthanasia should not, therefore, be taken at face value. Is the patient depressed, does he feel unwanted, does he feel a burden on his relatives, are his symptoms not being adequately controlled, is he the victim of meddlesome medicine, or is he fearful of future suffering that need not be if he is properly cared for? Almost certainly the answer to one of these questions will be in the affirmative.

Conclusion

To pursue legislation to allow voluntary euthanasia would be unwise when much of the supporting "evidence" derives from instances in which pain or other symptoms have been inadequately controlled and from the use of inappropriate treatments. Moreover, it is clear that society is far from unanimous on this issue, and to press forward with what can only be described as a divisive measure would inflict a severe strain upon the community.

Generally speaking, it is only in recent years that medical students have received instruction in the art of pain relief. This means that an account of a person dying in agony after weeks or months of unrelieved pain should increasingly become a thing of the past.

Legislation will not correct ignorance about the management of pain and other symptoms or about available supportive resources, nor will it stop meddlesome medicine. On the other hand, a positive approach to death by society in general together with compassionate, competent medical care and considerate, patient-oriented nursing will do much to overcome the present problems.

Ω

The Rights of Personhood

Death is social, we argued in the first pages of this volume. The critical social nature of death was seen initially in the social suicide. What difference did it make to the survivors of the social suicide to learn that the "deceased" was alive but living with others elsewhere? To the survivors the social suicide had died from their lives. They felt bereaved and considered themselves to be widows and widowers, survivors of the deceased.

From the point of view of those committing the social suicide, a death had also taken place. Who they were in terms of their families (husbands, fathers), who they were at work (physician, professor, developer), and what were the other roles constituting their social self also died upon their feigned death. Because they left those aspects of self behind, including their important certifying credentials, their identities also had died a death little less final than being under the ground.

Having introduced our theme, we then examined the circumstances under which people take their own physical lives. Implicit throughout the discussions on suicide was the argument that individuals assess the quality of their lives and at times find death preferable to some circumstances of life. Such circumstances may be as limited as those in which a secret agent is captured and prefers quick death to a slow death by torture. Whatever the circumstances may be, the essential point is that for many, life has a meaning beyond pure physical existence. For many if not for most of us, life to be human must have certain essential qualities. Persona we called it in our discussion of suicide, but how can the "essential qualities of life" be defined?

Medical authorities have now defined more precisely when death can be said to have occurred. Upon examining the topic, they found death to be most adequately conceptualized as a process having a number of stages, among them, organ death, brain death, and cellular death. Although the cells might be said to have "life," would one be considered "alive" if cellular life was the only life one had? What about someone who has been in a prolonged coma, sustained only by machines? Does "life" in its essential human qualities consist of anything more than the brain-wave patterns that the Harvard Medical School Committee said indicate the presence of "life"? Does human persona transcend purely physical existence?

We began with the theme that death is social, and perhaps now we are prepared to conceive that life is social, too. Perhaps we should view life as a process that, like death, has a number of stages. At the most basic level we could begin with brain-wave activity, what we might call cerebral life. If life is conceived as a process with various stages, perhaps we need not be forced to sustain life that exists only at the cerebral level. Brain-wave activity may be seen as a necessary but not sufficient condition for life. Death may be defined as the absence of brain waves, but the presence of brain waves need not signify life. That is, it must be assumed that something more than some gray matter discharging electrical impulses is necessary to constitute life. While some may perhaps be content with an occasional cerebral discharge, for nearly all of us, life means something far more.

Death is social and so is life. They are twin processes, each with its own series of stages. While physicians quite rightly define life in neurophysiological terms, we, as students of human behavior, must define it in human terms. Examining the rationality, the justifiability, and the typology of suicide led to the observation that for some people elective death is preferable to continued life under certain circumstances.

Does anyone ever have a right to make such a fateful choice? The editors of this volume have contended that everyone necessarily has that right as part of his or her freedom. To be free, we must be able to make the decisions that influence our lives and our deaths. If we do not have the ability to choose life or death, how much are our other choices impoverished? Socialists argue that the lives of citizens belong to the state. To commit suicide therefore constitutes a crime against the state. If one must then live or die as the state dictates, how much are the remaining choices worth?

We have argued that, under some circumstances, suicide must be accepted as rational and justified. We have argued that many people commit suicide because they are angry or feel worthless or because they lack control over their lives. It would be cruel to condone such acts because that would in effect justify the very imperfect status quo that produces them. Therefore, however desirous of death people may be, we would only mobilize society's agents of prevention, rehabilitation, and reform. Justification we would reserve for only one type of suicide, the one that involves a loss of persona. To cease to be one's self, voluntarily or because of forces outside one's control, is in fact to die. If one has already died socially, it is only right, proper, and dignified that the physical body should follow where the social self has already gone.

The contemplation of such circumstances is not pleasant. To envisage one's own social but not physical death may in fact be more unpleasant than imagining them occurring together. And the difficulties do not stop even there. Suppose the unthinkable happens. One finds that for reasons of old age or perhaps accident the social self is no more, but the body "lives" on. If able, one would commit suicide but is unable to do so. Thus does the issue of euthanasia become joined to that of suicide. And as with suicide we can accept it under certain circumstances. This is seen in a recent article by Sanders.

In an article published in 1977, Sanders analyzed the ten known prosecutions for euthanasia in the United States, ones performed by nonmedical persons. Of the ten, six were acquitted, one was not indicted, two were found guilty of a lesser degree of homicide, and one was convicted of first degree murder. The person convicted of first degree murder, however, had his death sentence commuted to life, then reduced, and was shortly thereafter paroled. In all the cases reviewed, the juries apparently felt, perhaps with good cause, that rehabilitation, retribution, or protection of society were not at issue.

From the foregoing data Sanders maintains that euthanasia should not be legalized because the evidence shows that the "present system . . . has not yet worked a great injustice on anyone committing euthanasia." Although his review of the cases that have been prosecuted substantiates his statement, his assumption that all acts of euthanasia are prosecuted or that no one fails to act given the present system undercuts his claim of no injustice.

Under what circumstances should suicide and euthanasia be accepted? At one extreme are those who would legitimate virtually whatever the individual wills. As wise students of human behavior know, at times people must be protected from themselves. Recall the pleas for death cited by Twycross that were reversed once pain had been adequately controlled. In addition, should not one be able to change his or her mind about such a fundamental matter? Clearly individual desire, while it must be taken into account, is insufficient as the sole basis for the acceptance of either suicide or euthanasia.

A second alternative is to place the decision solely in the hands of the physician. Although the following quote illustrates the point of view of one opposed to euthanasia, notice that he states he could perform such an act and presumably would if he believed it to be justifiable: "I have seen the true wish for death among my patients. . . . One must be able to say to them, I have listened—but the consequences for humanity are such that though I could open the door and let you out, others may then be thrown out" (Auer, 1977). There are also conflicts of interest between patient and physician, between family and patient, between patient and hospital, between transplant recipient and donor and such conflicts further underscore the importance of considering elective death in a larger context than the individual or physician alone.

The study of previous efforts to deal with these difficult questions is often instructive. By studying legislative philosophy, intent, and consequences, we can learn how better to decide in the present. Therefore we turn now to Eser's contribution to this volume.

"Sanctity" and "Quality" of Life in a Historical-Comparative View

by Albin Eser

There has always been some discussion of whether it is worthwhile at all to compare the institutions, the legal codes, and other traditions of different countries. Yet, even if some areas do not admit comparisons, there is at least one that is of universal significance: the value and protection of human life. If there is one value that is universal, that could truly be called "holy," then it is human life. This is conceded even by those who, as agnostics, are far from arguing on religious grounds. Glanville Williams, for example, once president of the English Euthanasia Society, stated in his famous book *The Sanctity of Life* (1958:30) that even by the "modern infidel" it is widely accepted to be "our duty to regard all human life as sacred, however disabled, worthless or even repugnant the individual may be."

Yet it is not only this universal appreciation of life that makes comparisons possible and necessary between states and nations. An even stronger reason today is the presumption that there has been no time in the history of mankind in which life has been more endangered. If we think of environmental pollution, the proliferation of nuclear warfare, and chemical contamination, we must get the impression that human life is not an absolute value but only one among other interests of our society. And if we turn from these more or less unintended devaluations of human life to the intentional taking of life, as happens in capital punishment, abortion, suicide, and euthanasia, it might appear that the sanctity of life is merely an ideal and not truly a moral or legal obligation.

The *sanctity of life* is one approach taken in the rationale for the legal protection of life. Within this approach life is considered as a value per se. It is considered to be worth protecting regardless of any physical or mental deficiencies and regardless of the social utility of life. Conflicting with the sanctity-of-life approach are tendencies within society that might be broadly characterized as a *quality-of-*

life approach. Within this approach, life must have certain qualities; existing physically is not sufficient. Further, life might be abandoned if it lost certain physical, mental, or social qualities, when the individual did not deem it worthwhile to live any longer.

Each of these two general approaches has its own moral rationale. Since this rationale is evident in a society's legal code, by comparing codes we can learn how and why various societies have sought to protect life. Such knowledge can perhaps inform our contemporary debate.

The protection of life given in the first nationwide German penal code, the so-called Carolina, will be examined first because of its widespread influence. This code, which was developed in the age of the Lutheran reformation, will then be compared to the protection of life in contemporary penal law. This focus will be upon the moral rationale behind the law, rather than upon its structural technicalities.

The Carolina Code of 1532

In 1532 the Holy Roman Empire of German Nation enacted its first imperial penal code under Emperor Charles V, for whom it was named in Latin *Constitutio Criminalis Carolina.* The Carolina was valid in a substantial part of continental Europe for almost 350 years, until 1871. It represented a crystallization of the discriminatory protection of life in the old Roman law, the gradual evaluation of life in the Germanic laws, and the sanctity of life as derived from the ethics of ecclesiastical canon law. This evaluation of life can be demonstrated by looking at some particularly crucial points in the protection of life, including abortion, so-called monster killing, suicide, euthanasia, and punishment by death.

As far as the protection of life in principle is concerned, in the Carolina Code there are no provisions discriminating between certain qualities of human beings, with the exception of abortion and monster killing. Any individual was treated as a person, without any caveat about age, physical or mental quality, sex, or social status. This code represented substantial progress over the old Roman law in which men were not necessarily equal. Under Roman law, for example, murder was restricted to the killing of a *homo liber,* a free man or citizen (Festus, 1899:612; *"Si qui hominen liberum morti duit, parricidas esto"*). Since slaves were not considered to be human beings but merely chattel, the killing of a slave was punishable only as the destruction of property. Since the master could destroy his own property, as a matter of course, the statute would punish only for the killing of another man's slave (Mommsen, 1899). Thus in Roman law human life was not recognized as a worth in itself but according to the social role of the individual. This status-oriented discrimination declined only somewhat with Emperor Constantine in the fourth century after Christ.

Similarly, under the German tribal laws, the unfree servant was not considered to be a person, but only a movable chattel, subject to the master's power, which included the right of killing (Schmidt, 1965:260). This status-oriented evaluation of life continued into the medieval compensation system, by which the sum paid for murder or manslaughter was differentiated by age, sex, and status. The medieval system also took into account a woman's ability to bear children and whether the slain had been baptized (Rosshirt, 1839:194).

The progress of the Carolina in protecting all life alike was therefore considerable. It is explainable in part by the growing influence of Christian thinking, which views life as a gift of God (Aquinas, 1266:165). As a creature of God, any human being, by its very existence, is fundamentally equal to any other. As Dietrich Bonhoeffer puts it: "The fact that God is the creator, maintainer, and redeemer of man, that makes even the most miserable life worth living" (1949:108). Without regard to any physical quality or social status, human life is per se sacred and intangible.

This spiritualized view of life found its way into the Carolina, as can be observed with respect to abortion and infanticide. Whereas life is physically apprehensible and thereby its protection more easily comprehensible, respect for unborn life requires more sophistication. Additional extension is necessary to take the position that the right to life is not necessarily dependent upon the ability of "standing on one's own feet." The right to life may also be attributed to a person who, although not yet fully developed, at least represents all genetic elements of an individualized entity.

Under Roman law abortion was not punished, although it was considered an indecency. When abuse of it by the upper classes finally led to punishment for abortion, the rationale was cast in terms of demographic policy rather than protection of life (Spangenberg, 1818). Roman law also contained provisions to protect the father. That is, abortion was treated as an attack against the father because he was deprived of his legitimate descendants (Eser, 1977a).

Contrary to this Roman (and basically Greek) attitude, the Germanic laws of the Middle Ages are characterized by an increasing engagement of the protection of unborn life (Eser, 1977a). This development, too, cannot be explained except by the influence of the Church, in particular by the Christian notion of the soul: if the soul is essential for being "man," the protection of life naturally cannot merely be centered in the state of the body or in the body's utility to society. The anima, or soul, also must be respected. This new theological-anthropological concept furthered three consequences.

First, the protection of unborn life was strengthened and institutionalized. If the soul is an essential part of the individual and if the embryo already has a soul, then the embryo deserves protection from the time of having gained a soul. Further, it must be protected not just as part of the mother but by virtue of its own right as a person already genetically defined and individualized (Rosshirt, 1839).

Second, it seems quite certain that within this doctrine the sanctity-of-life principle has its origin. If man is enabled by his soul to participate in divine life, as a body and soul entity, he is entering within the sphere of holiness.

Third, certain restrictions in the protection of life also followed. If only the person with soul deserves protection, this protection may be withheld from those who could be denied as having souls. Thus, protection could be withheld from the embryo in the first stage of pregnancy and from the so-called monster (Hinschius, 1888:31, 47).

All three of these developments are evident within the Carolina. Abortion was declared to equal the killing of a born person (Wächter, 1829), and thereby the fetus was endowed with an independent right to life. On the other hand, the Carolina differentiated between the abortion of a "living" versus a "nonliving" child. In the latter case the punishment was at the discretion of the court, but in the former, decapitation was mandatory. By reason of this differentiation, the criterion of being alive* became a controversial point for a long time. Whereas some tried to interpret *alive* in the sense of *viable* (Spangenberg, 1818), the prevailing opinion in German jurisprudence interpreted *alive* in the sense of being endowed with a soul, that is, animated.

The German courts then had to decide when animation took place. Partly by invoking Aristotle who considered an embryo as animated from the ninetieth day of pregnancy, partly by misinterpreting a Mosaic source that seemed to concede to the male fetus an animation twice as quick as that of a female fetus, the courts came to regard the fortieth day of pregnancy as the decisive moment of animation.

On the other hand, we should not disregard the crucial backside of the animation concept because it made the killing of a monster permissible. This was certainly consistent since creatures, presumably not having souls, were not considered persons and therefore were not covered by the statutes governing the protection of human life. Thus, the sanctity-of-life principle as such was not compromised. Yet, the cost lay in preserving theoretical consistency by excluding deficient beings from the notion of "man." Therefore, at least in this single instance, it becomes evident that even within the framework of Christian thinking of that time, life is sacred not because it exists but only insofar as it has a certain quality, that is, the quality of animation.

Until now we have dealt mainly with the protection of life at its beginning. We should also take a look at its protection from willful ending.

As far as the taking of life by suicide is concerned, the Carolina distinguished between two types. Criminals who attempted to avoid punishment by suicide were sanctioned by the confiscation of their property, which deprived the heirs of their expected inheritance. There was no sanction, however, for the suicide committed in the course of disease, depression, or similar other defects of free will. Since suicide was generally disapproved by the Church (Aqui-

*This was the criterion used by the U.S. Supreme Court (*Roe* v. *Wade*, 1973: 410).

nas, 1266: 9–11, 23, 5), however, the silence of the Carolina was used by various states to enact laws prohibiting all suicides and declaring attempted suicide and complicity a criminal act (Wächter, 1829).

There are no specific statements concerning euthanasia in the Carolina. This absence of any justifying or mitigating rules can be interpreted as rejecting any attempts to withdraw protection from human life, even if the individual concerned might wish to die (Simson and Geerdo, 1969).

If this were the entire picture of life protection in the Carolina, it might appear that life was considered an almost absolute and intangible value. If we also look at the various justifications rendering the killing of a human being legal, however, we find that the wall for protecting life is filled with quite a few holes, including justified killing in war, deadly self-defense, and especially the excessive use of punishment by death.

A number of theories of forfeiture have attempted to reconcile the death penalty with the sanctity of life and even proposed that execution protects life. Nevertheless, it can scarcely be denied that the imposition of death deprives life of its absolute intangibility, especially if capital punishment is sanctioned for retribution of interests other than life, as it is in the Carolina for blasphemy, sorcery, money clipping, rape, treason, arson, robbery, or burglary (Carolina: 106, 109, 111, 116, 119 ff.). In some of these circumstances, life is sacrificed for purely material interests. Whether such punishment is legitimate is not the question. Rather, any such justifications suspend the sanctity of life. The taboo of the "holiness" of life is touched; life becomes commensurate and subject to balancing against other interests. Its tangibility is turned into a relative rather than absolute character. As if to demonstrate this relativity, the Middle Ages with almost criminal imagination developed a number of shuddering aggravations of the death penalty: execution by drowning, burning, or burying alive, by breaking on the wheel or quartering (Carolina: 192).

In sum, the protection of life in one of the most influential penal codes in human history was rather disunited. As Williams observed, "Our forefathers were so solicitous for the dead that they sometimes forgot all decency and humanity to the living" (Williams, 1958). Ensuring the protection of life through the taking of life meant that the claim of sanctity was suspended. Allowing life to be sacrificed in favor of other interests made life a value that might be counterbalanced by others.

The Present Law and Its Tendencies

If we try to compare the protection of life by the Carolina with present law, we can observe some remarkable developments. As a matter of principle in present German law, life ranges as the highest of all human and social values. As the Federal Constitutional Court has stated, life is "the vital basis of human dignity and the prerequisite of all other fundamental rights." This high estimation of life is also expressed in the constitutional banning of the death penalty, as well as the fact that lifelong imprisonment is mandatory only in cases of murder in the first degree.

Life as a biological-sociological entity that deserves protection in each of its phases, without regard to individual feelings or social esteem, is a notion that had been expressed in the official comment to the Bavarian penal code of 1813 by Anselm Feuerbach, one of the greatest German criminalists: "That an embryo as well as a hoary old man or invalid expecting his death, or a criminal convicted to death, and similarly all human beings without distinction as to their nation, religion, status or age can be the subject of a crime of killing, this is expressed by the word 'man' (*Mensch*)." If everybody has the same right to life, one life cannot be balanced against another. Thus, in a case in which a person can rescue his own life only by sacrificing that of another, he may perhaps be excused on subjective grounds, but the act remains, since not justifiable, objectively wrongful (Lencker, 1978).

It is obvious that such an almost absolute postulate must have a number of restrictive consequences for such areas as abortion and euthanasia. Therefore the even more important question is the extent to which this principle is carried through the code, or in which instances the guarantee of life is somehow restricted. Therefore we need to examine particular provisions of present German law.

The death penalty has been completely abolished in Germany. To kill another in self-defense, as well as in war, is held legal (Eser, 1980). Although this will probably never be changed – since the recommendation of Christ to offer the other cheek may be a good rule of ethics but is not enforceable in law—we should at least be concerned by the fact that the effect of nuclear weapons is measured by "megadeaths."

Whereas we have discussed cases in which killing is somehow a reaction to some illegal attack, we now have to consider cases in which the killed person by no means can be called an aggressor but merely a victim: abortion, suicide, and euthanasia. In both Germany and the United States there is perhaps no question more controversial than the legality of abortion. Although the various codes since the Carolina have differed about when the fetus should be protected, the fundamental recognition of unborn life as such has remained unchanged in principle. Even Germany's abortion reform act of 1974 by which pregnancy could be interrupted in the first three months if the mother had obtained certain counseling procedures did not touch this principle. Because this statute allowed abortion without requiring a specific justification, it was invalidated by the Federal Constitutional Court. On this issue the German "supreme court" reached just the opposite conclusion as the United States Supreme Court. Whereas the American court denied the fetus its own right of life prior to its viability, the German court held that the right to life that is guaranteed to everyone by the constitution is also guaranteed to the fetus as a person by virtue of its own right to life, independent from the will or interest of the mother. Therefore the German legislature was forced to draft a new reform bill by which the embryo by virtue of its own right to life is protected and abortion is allowed only in cases in which the mother can prove a prevailing counterinterest (New German Penal Code: 218a).

The history of the recognition of such counterinterests has quite typically grown in combination with increases in the protection of unborn life. Such antagonistic development between the sanctity and the quality of life is quite typical. To review just briefly some of the developments regarding counterinterests, we should begin with Germany's landmark decision of 1927 by which abortion in order to save the life or health of the mother was recognized, the so-called medical indication as objective justification (Eser, 1976a). This was followed in the 1930s by the so-called eugenic indication that allowed for no place in the National Socialist society for "deficient" life (Schönke, 1942:447). As with the Carolina, the justification offered, whether racist, demographic, or "altruistic," matters not in terms of the sacrifices thus made of the sanctity-of-life principle. Recognizing eugenic grounds for killing a fetus holds life sacred only when it passes some social-hygenic quality test. No less questionable from a sanctity-of-life approach is the present recognition of the so-called social indication by which a pregnancy may be interrupted.

Certainly there are good human reasons as well as legal ways to justify the prevailing interests of the mother. In the context of sanctity versus quality of life, however, there is no doubt that at least unborn life is degraded to a level that can be counterbalanced even by purely material interests: the mother's *quality* of life prevails over the child's *existence* of life.

The principle of the sanctity of life becomes even more severely tested when we turn to the protection of the so-called *monstrum*. Whereas abortion can at least be explained by counterinterests of the mother, the killing of the deformed puts the quality of human life at stake. As we noted, the Carolina was consistent in that it held that such creatures lacked souls and therefore protection of life did not include them. Since this notion was revoked even by the Catholic Church in the nineteenth century (Hinschius, 1893:798), today we cannot kill in a similar "conscience of innocence." Particularly in Germany, such killings were completely discredited by the "euthanasia actions" of the National Socialist regime. We also realize that any line drawn between the "normal" and the "abnormal" is of necessity arbitrary and without empirical foundation (Schowing, 1974:2).

On the other hand, it is quite obvious that a severely physically or mentally deficient individual, if not relieved by merciful death, will have a difficult life and be a burden to the family. For this reason, there is a great temptation to deny such life the quality of being human. Such thinking allows killing "it" at birth or at least refraining from life-preserving measures as is done in quite a few hospitals (Heifetz, 1976). There is no apparent solution, but what must be fully recognized is the fundamental significance of such thinking or practice. If we were to concede that human life is constituted not merely by physical existence but rather by the normality of the body, the degree of mental capacity, the ability of self-maintenance, or by some social utility, we certainly would cross the Rubicon to a finally qualitative evaluation of human life. Perhaps some day this step might turn out to be unavoidable. It would be catastrophic to the protection of life, however, if this step were taken without sincere and open consideration of the fundamental moral and constitutional problems involved. The experience of Germany in the Third Reich testifies to the potential for tragedy in this regard.

Finally turning to the other end of the life cycle, let us briefly examine some of the most controversial problems at stake. As far as voluntary passive euthanasia is concerned—that is, the withholding of treatment on the patient's consent or even demand—no new legal regulations are needed, since it is the patient's right to refuse treatment even though this may consequently lead to the patient's death. At least in principle this right is unquestioned (Eser, 1977). Therefore a natural death act (like that in California) might perhaps be clarifying but is not essential.

Where the real problems begin—and where even the natural death acts fall short since they cover only euthanasia by consent—is where the true will of the patient cannot be evaluated, either because of unconsciousness or because the patient cannot be confronted with the question of whether treatment should go on. If toward this involuntary letting die we were to maintain a pure sanctity-of-life approach, all life-preserving measures—at any cost and up to the last breath—would be a compelling command. Yet the question is whether this would be a true help. Whereas active killing of human life is prohibited per se, letting a person die is only unlawful if there is some legal duty to act. Therefore the main question is how much an individual may reasonably expect from society as far as what should be done to preserve that person's life. The answer has to be given with regard to the function of medical care. Since medical treatment as a social action is primarily designed to preserve or produce the individual's ability of self-consciousness and self-realization, the physician's duty to maintain vegetative life comes to an end when there is not the slightest hope any more for the patient's regaining consciousness.

So far this criterion has nothing to do with the question of costs; it is simply based on the social function of medicine to preserve human self-realization. Even here it must be recognized that medical practice is increasingly going beyond this line, either by using dying patients for experimental purposes or by terminating treatment for financial reasons. It is quite clear that by such an external balancing of life against other interests, the sanctity-of-life road again is left.

Such compromises are even more the case when we consider the tension between the protection of life and the right of self-determination as it appears in suicide and killing on demand. Again, sanctity and quality of life are at issue. Sanctity is involved insofar as life is considered a social value to be protected even if the individual does not think or wish so. Quality is involved insofar as an individual believes that certain conditions in life are so essential that, without them, life loses its worthiness and suicide or active euthanasia is called for. In this self-determination of life and death is the most radical postulation of a qualitative conception of life.

The legal recognition of self-determination has had a rather divergent development in Germany. The Carolina punished killing on demand as it did any other homicide, but by the middle of the eighteenth century mitigating provisions were made. The result is that German law today handles killing on demand in a special provision (S 216) that provides a much milder sanction than for any other killing. The notion, however, that killing on demand should not be penalized at all has not been accepted by German legislation to date, and with good reason. Not only is the fear of abuse certainly a serious one, but an even more serious concern is that killing on demand is not an act of pure self-determination; the last decision about life or death is left to another person. Yet, although killing on demand does withdraw from life its taboo of intangibility, it should not necessarily be punishable. A person who renders active euthanasia on demand might perhaps be excepted from punishability on personal grounds, but the killing, in terms of its objective unlawfulness, cannot be justified.

Although there has been a mitigating tendency toward killing on demand, the development of the various codes with respect to suicide has been less straightforward. After some restrained disapproval in the Carolina, suicide became subject increasingly to severe condemnation in common law practice (Simson, 1967). One of the most famous scholars and judges of the eighteenth century, Benedict Carpzow, did not hesitate to deem the suicide guilty of double murder, since he both destroyed his body and corrupted his soul (Wächter, 1829). Even such an enlightened legal scholar as Feuerbach (1826) found suicide unlawful because the subject deprived the state of his abilities. On the other hand, the Prussian Penal Code of 1794 abstained from punishing attempted suicide, on the grounds that such a person would deserve only mercy. Participation in suicide, however, continued to be punishable. This is still the state of suicide law in quite a few European countries, such as Austria (S 78) and Switzerland (S 115).

In Germany, however, the nonpunishability of suicide as well as of the participation in it was well established by the middle of the nineteenth century. The rationale for this rather liberal view was that one cannot stand in a legal relationship to oneself and therefore cannot commit a wrongful act toward the self; neither can another participate in it. This rationale is valid, of course, only if the suicide is really an act of free will. Thus, whether there is a free will to die becomes the controversial point. As some argue that suicidal wishes are generally influenced by personal or circumstantial factors excluding free will, there is a growing movement at least to punish the instigator of a suicide, if not also anyone who aids (Geilen, 1974:147).

In spite of these uncertainties, the decision of German law not to interfere with suicide by criminal sanctions is, in principle, correct. As we have already indicated, suicide is the case in point for the conflict between sanctity-oriented protection of life and quality-motivated self-determination. Were we to give the sanctity principle absolute priority, a person longing for death would be degraded to an object doomed to live for the exclusive interest of the state. If we do not want to apotheosize the state as a life-giving divinity, we scarcely can deny the power of every person over his or her living and dying (Eser, 1976b:392).

Conclusion

If we had to draw conclusions from the changing development in the legal history of life protection, the main observation would be that even such a supreme good as life can neither exclusively be protected by sanctity commands nor be given over only to quality aspects. Both sanctity and quality principles must be brought into an optimum of concordance. On the one hand, the sanctity of life must not somehow become so rigid that the longing of the actual human being for a meaningful life might be subdued. On the other hand, in the longing for quality of life the primary prerequisite of existence should not get undermined. This is particularly important when not one's own but another's life is at stake. If, for instance, unborn life that is undesired or expiring life that is not adequately cared for is supposed to not get born or to be better off dead, we then prevail with our own quality conceptions over their existential ones. To say "Oh, we only mean well for you" can be pretension to secure the better for oneself. Egoism in the mantle of humanism—this, too, is a danger from which life must be protected.

Ω

Toward a Good Death

The good life is pursued and valued by nearly everyone, and although we may not like to think of it and may avoid thinking about it entirely, we also would like to have a good death. When we think about death, we say we hope we will go quickly, without pain, before or after someone else. In these and various other ways we indicate what constitutes a good death for us.

While we plan and work for the good life, we tend to leave our manner of death to chance. A good life is something the living person experiences in the process of living, and a good death is something the dying person experiences in the process of dying. The kind of death we die, like the kind of life we live, however, depends in part on how we work and plan for it. It is our hope that readers of this book will be encouraged to become involved in their own lives and their own deaths. We have discussed suicide and euthanasia in an effort to engage our readers in the contemporary dialogue so that they will be able to reach an informed decision about the way they will die.

Our discussion would fall short, however, were we not to consider what individuals can do to implement their own decisions with respect to these issues. While one may have decided that, with respect to one's own death, heroic measures are not to be pursued, the decision does not matter if the attending physician or one's own relatives think otherwise. In "A Legal Structure for the Living Will," Frank Marsh outlines the measures that must be enacted to assure the right of all persons to die their own deaths.

A Legal Structure for the Living Will

by Frank H. Marsh

Within the fields of bioethics and of law, one of the more controversial issues is certainly that of determining a practical legal procedure for implementing the performance of a dying patient's moral right to die. At present, we must contend with a ponderous and almost endless legal maze in order to satisfy an unconscious terminal patient's wish to die. We have only to turn to the *Quinlan* case and the more recent *Northern* case to understand the magnitude of the legal complexities surrounding any attempt to enforce a patient's right to die. While some states have enacted "right-to-die" laws, these laws only establish the criteria for determining the presence or absence of brain death or when a patient can be declared legally dead. They do not provide for any legal response to the right-to-die issue.

In discussions concerning the right-to-die issue, some philosophers, physicians, and lawyers have suggested that a legally enforceable "living will" could provide the necessary procedure for enforcing the moral right to die. However, there are many questions that can be raised about the performance of a living will. Who will "pull the plug" or carry out the instructions of the will? How will the document be made known and probated with the court? Will the constitutional right of due process be satisfied? Will the physician or hospital incur legal liability for failure to heed the directions of the will? How much time must elapse before invoking and probating the will, once the applicable medical conditions have been determined? All of these questions are important in demonstrating some of the complexities surrounding the operation of a living will and the obvious mandatory procedures by which it is to become operative. In the following sections of this chapter, a positive and protective procedure for implementing the living will is presented, as well as answers to the above questions and certain others that might be raised.

For the purposes of discussion, we will restrict the applicability of the living will to those extreme cases in which there is the need and the desire for escape from a medically imposed prolongation of biological life within the human body. The proposed action will be legally restricted to cases involving brain damage (from any source) and resulting irreversible coma and to the terminally ill or aged patient who has passed into the initial stages of a death coma. The argument as presented will focus on a method of expressing moral consent, acceptable at law, to allow medically administered euthanasia, either actively through the administering of drugs or passively through the withdrawal of life-supportive measures. Because of its application to the unconscious life, the living will cannot be utilized when a person is mortally wounded but remains conscious to the moment of expiration, or when a person is terminally ill or aged but has not passed into a coma or permanently lost sensibility or rationality. The living will can be invoked only in the ultimate and extreme medical case.

There is in existence at this time, under the Tennessee Code (34–1008) and other state codes, a very simple but adequate court procedure for the appointment of a conservator for an individual who is unable to care for himself or herself or any property because of advanced age or medical disability. It is basically a legal method whereby the court-appointed party, generally a member of the immediate family, can protect and administer the assets and estate of another person. The court here recognizes that under certain conditions an individual might become so incapacitated as to be unable to care for himself or herself and see to the ordinary business affairs of a person's life. The procedure followed is for the family or a friend to file with the probate court a petition setting forth the immediate need for a conservator and to request a prompt hearing on the matter. A guardian *ad litem* is duly appointed by the court to represent the incapacitated person in the court proceeding and a medical examination by two physicians is directed. At the court hearing, the testimonies of the moving party and witnesses are required as evidence of the individual's condition, along with the statement of the examining doctors. Rarely, if ever, does the incapacitated individual appear in person before the court but is present through the court-appointed guardian *ad litem.*

While it would be pretentious to imply at this time that there can be a comparison between the proceeding described for the appointment of a conservator and the anticipated procedure for terminating a life under a living will, this procedure is outlined to indicate a case in which a recognized legal procedure is currently being employed to protect basic property rights when the individual cannot do so. The performance by the court is the promotion and implementation of an assumed intent assigned to the incapacitated person —that one would so act to protect one's property and other rights if one were able. It should be pointed out that the contrary intent is possible, that the actions of a court-appointed conservator might very well be opposite from what the ward's desires are; however, these actions should be for the best interest of the ward. For example, a conservator might determine that it is best to sell a portfolio of stock in a declining market, whereas the ward desires to keep the stock even though there would be a depreciation of the estate. To some extent there is a disenfranchisement of property rights.

For a comparative study of similar state codes authorizing a like conservatorship action, we will group the conditions necessary for the validation of a living will under the following topics: notice, service of process, evidence, time or duration, and court-directed enforcement. In addition, there are, of course, the nonconditional requirements in the construction of the document itself. This is an element necessary for validation of the will, but since it is separate and apart from the actual proceeding, it will be dealt with first.

Nonconditional Requirements

As in the instance of uniform will statutes, there are certain specific statutory prerequisites that are mandatory for declaring any will valid. These are the obvious points dealing with the presence or absence of the testator's signature and that of two attesting witnesses, and the particular form of instrument. The living will must be prefaced with a declaration, as required in a last will and testament, that the testator is competent and sound of mind, of lawful age, and that it is to be the testator's living will. The living will could begin, "I, John Doe, being of sound mind and of lawful age, do hereby make this to be my last living will."

Secondly, the body of the will must enunciate the testator's intentions, qualifications, and limits, and it must be capable of being performed. This is to say, by comparing a last will and testament, if one were to bequeath the sum of $1 million to one's next of kin, while in reality the total estate amounted to no more than $500, there could be no performance. In order to satisfy this requirement, the body of a living will must be so qualified and structured to satisfy the particular statutes establishing the legal right to die. Requiring a performance under a living will of anything less than or equal to that established by statute would automatically void the will.

Thirdly, the will must be executed by the patient in the presence of two competent adult witnesses who are of no kin and who will not benefit in any way from the patient's death. A similar restrictive measure (Tennessee SS 32–101–108) is imposed upon a last will and testament. As in the last will, the two witnesses to the living will must know the patient and without reservation indicate, by the affixation of their signatures to the will, their declaration and affirmation of the patient's soundness of mind and rationality at the time of his signing. Both the attesting witnesses must affix their signatures in the presence of each other and in the presence of the testator, whose signing must be in the presence of both witnesses together.

Due to the very subject matter and the extensive safeguards necessary for protection of life and the integrity of the will, an instrument that does not follow the prescribed procedure must be disallowed. There can be no exceptions. It is proposed, then, that any legislative act establishing the right to a living will use the following form:

> I, John Doe, being of sound mind and of lawful age, do hereby make and declare this to be my living will.
>
> If the situation should ever arise in which there is no reasonable expectation of my recovery from an unconscious state or coma, regardless of its cause, be it disease, old age, or accident, I direct that I be allowed to die immediately either through termination of any artificial measures if they are being employed or through direct administering of painless medication.

This directive will is not made out of any duress or coercion, but of my own free will and conviction.

Executed this ________ day of ________, 19____.

____
Testator

We, the undersigned, as witnesses to the living will of ________________ hereby attest that ________________ did execute this instrument to be his living will, in our presence, and believing him to be of sound mind and competent to execute same, we so affixed our signatures here as attesting witnesses, signing in the presence of each other and in the presence of the testator.

____
Witness

____
Witness

We have purposely limited the applicability of the document to the irreversible coma. However, it is sometimes held—and it is arguable—that the living will could be extended by the enabling statute to include a condition of physical brain damage or mental deterioration in which normal faculties are severely and irreparably impaired and in which life can be maintained indefinitely by artificial means.

As an element of the necessary restrictive measures, the question of soundness, rationality, and free will must be considered by the court in its deliberations during the probate of the will and must be irrefutable evidentiary facts. This is not as difficult as it might appear on first impression. The testimony of the two attesting witnesses will suffice unless contested, and if it is contested, the issue of competency or free will must be decided by the court. The court at this time would also determine if there has been a revocation of the will, either in writing by the testator or through a verbal declaration of his intent to a disinterested party prior to lapsing into a coma. Any serious reservations retained in the mind of the court on these issues would negate the will.

We will now proceed to the court procedure necessary for probating and administering the living will. It is here that the rights of both the patient and society will be ultimately protected and realized.

Notice and Service of Process

The conditions of notice and service of process are often erroneously assumed to be the same. This assumption is derived generally from cases in which the parties in litigation must be notified of all events taking place in their impending cases. Notice and service are, however, two distinct conditions, both of which must be met and fully satisfied before there can be any commencement of probation. In any type of court proceeding there will be two groups involved – what the law (Tennessee C.P.R. 17:02) defines as interested parties and necessary parties. A necessary party is what the term denotes, a party that must be before the court for jurisdictional purposes and that will be bound by the finding of the court. The applicability of any court decree is usually extended only to the necessary parties and no further. While service of process is required on all necessary parties, only notice of any probable litigation is required for interested parties. For example, in the case of a last will and testament, notice to the executor's surety might be necessary to keep it informed of the proceedings.

An interested party cannot contest the validity of the testator's will. Such a party does not have official standing before the court unless brought before the court through an intervening petition. Generally, this party's presence is not critical to a determination by the court, whereas each necessary party's presence is. Through notice, an interested party would be made aware of a living will and of the party's right to indicate any objections by intervening as indicated. There is precedent (C.P.R. 22:01) for this type of procedure.

In the case of a living will, who will be the necessary parties and who the interested parties? The presence of a host of necessary parties would make the procedure both cumbersome and expensive and should be avoided. Thus the necessary parties will be limited to those persons whose direct rights and counter-rights are involved. This would include the patient, the hospital, the attending physician in charge of treatment measures, and the patient's spouse when he or she is married or the immediate next of kin (only parents or children) if the patient is unmarried or if the spouse is incompetent. Immediately after the living will is filed for probate, the court will appoint a guardian *ad litem* to appear and represent the patient as a necessary party. This procedure is similar to the conservatorship proceedings (Tennessee Code 34–1008). At the time of the filing, notice shall be served upon all other doctors who have treated or are treating the patient in consultation with the attending physician. This notice will permit any one of these doctors either to voice any objections that the doctor might have or to voice an agreement if so desired.

In addition to the notice sent to the other doctors, a notice of the filing of the will shall be sent to the attorney general's office in the county of the probate. The attorney general acts as a representative of society's interest in what is proposed. The attorney general is empowered to maintain a representative on behalf of the state at all hearings and to have unlimited access to all court files kept on the proceedings. This participation by the state should have a sobering effect on any possible intended violations of the right to die.

It should be pointed out that since either a member of the family or a representative of the hospital must initiate the probation of the will, the moving party need not be served with process separately. Most petitions to the court for probate will be filed jointly by the family and the hospital, and this concurrent effort will lend considerable strength to the ultimate judgment on the validity of a patient's will.

The Evidence

We will now turn to the critical area of the proposed procedures, the evidence necessary to substantiate a judicial decree affirming the living will and, by way of injunctive order, to direct the relief sought. There are two distinct factual conditions that must be satisfied, and a failure in either would negate the entire proceeding. These are (1) adult competency and (2) an irreversible unconscious state. Thus, the will must fail in either of the following situations: one could be found to be competent but in a medical state of unconscious limbo, as in the *Quinlan* case, or one could have total brain death in accord with AMA standards but have had questioned competency at the time the will was executed. Under the first situation, however, the court could very well reserve its decision for any medical recall should the unconscious state of the patient become irreversible. For example, the condition of adult competency might be satisfied in a given case, but a clear and final prognosis of the patient's condition be unable to be made. Rather than dismiss the petition of probate, the court could, at its discretion, withhold any judgment for a reasonable period of time in order to ascertain if the unconscious state of the patient will be declared irreversible.

Obviously, the first condition (adult competency) will be the easiest requirement to satisfy. Generally in any proceeding in which competency is a requirement, the court does not presuppose a state of incompetency but maintains a neutral opinion. If the family is the moving party, the simple reaffirmation of competency (*Bartee* v. *Thompson*, 67:508) by the attesting witnesses to the will is sufficient proof. If the condition of competency is placed in issue, the court would then have to make this determination before a consideration of the medical condition could be entertained. There is no need to elaborate on what is necessary for establishing the competency of a patient; this is a legal evidentiary fact for the court to decide on the basis of the weight and credibility of the evidence offered. Because of the timing granted to the execution of a will, it is fair to assume that the condition of competency will be more likely uncontested than contested (*Kirkpatrick* v. *Kirkpatrick*, 61:342). The contestable circumstances would be expected when a patient is facing death from a terminal illness and executed a will within one or two days prior to lapsing into an unconscious state. An individual suffering from the ravages of extreme pain or advanced senility of age could not be expected to be rational in signing such a will.

It is in the second condition set forth that we can expect the most controversy to emerge. Will the attending physician and hospital support the family's position? First of all, it must be recognized that the evidence to be introduced during this phase of the trial must, by necessity, be highly technical and expert testimony. The family and other lay parties can do nothing. After the introduction of all medical testimony and hospital records, the problem must resolve itself to one final question and affirmative answer by the attending physician.

Q. Doctor, do you have an opinion about the finality and permanence of Mary Jane's unconscious state?

A. Yes.

Q. Please state that opinion.

A. It is permanent and irreversible.

Anything short of this response by the doctor would introduce contested probabilities for the court to decide between. One could expect the above answer by the attending physician if, and only if, there were a unanimity of opinion among all physicians connected in some way with the case. If there were questions raised by any of these medical parties, these questions would be made available to the court; and the court, if unable to decide the issue, could appoint an independent medical evaluation team composed of the necessary relevant specialists. This team of specialists would be required to make an immediate inquiry into the questioned case and render a written decision to the court on the permanency or nonpermanency of the unconscious state. There is precedence (Tennessee Code 50:1018–25) for this type of evidentiary investigation and evaluation. If there is any question left to the court that would create a reasonable doubt, the condition must fail and the will be negated. This area of the proceedings must remain highly flexible since the patient's condition in an unconscious state might stabilize such that a determination could be made to the court's satisfaction.

In the preceding paragraph, the term *reasonable doubt* was employed. This term denotes the degree to which the weight of evidence must go for the court to act. There are other degrees of evidence that fall on a continuum. At one end we find the standard weight of evidence applied in the vast majority of civil litigations, the necessity to establish a case by a bare preponderance of the evidence. This is the evidence that will tip an imaginary scale one way or the other (*Hull* v. *Evans*, 59:193). The objections to the use of this degree in living will cases are obvious, and no argument need be interposed here. At the opposite end of the continuum is the standard required in all criminal cases, that the evidence must be beyond a "reasonable doubt." Because of the very nature of the living will in dealing with life itself, no less a standard should be employed than the identical one being used at this time to make a determination of guilt in a capital offense with resulting deprivation of life. "Beyond reasonable doubt" is simply an evidentiary state that a reasonable person attains through consideration of the reasonableness of the facts being offered in evidence. In considering the case of a living will, the permanency of an irreversible coma would not be ascertained in terms of the possibility of recall, but in terms of an assumption of reasonableness versus unreasonableness that it might occur. Anything more or less would seriously jeopardize the thin line separating the two rights, the right to live and the right to die. The strictness of the standard of evidence would also dismiss any anxious arguments that the living will might open a Pandora's box of "slippery slope" arguments. On the other hand, it is recognized that requiring this strong degree of evidence could deny some patients their right to die. However, this is a necessary denial of utility in an unknown percentage of cases in order to protect the greater number from any possible wrongdoing or negation of their rights.

Time Limitations and Hearing

The final two conditions should present no serious problems. The time limitation or requirement is important in specifying when an action could be commenced and in securing the rapidity of handling the probate by the court. Since the underlying thesis of a living will is found within an extreme medical condition—that of a purported irreversible unconscious state with an undeterminable duration—an immediate and timely filing is necessary. After an initial opinion is rendered by an attending physician, forty-eight hours must pass before any filing of a will would be permitted. The reason for this is obvious, as an extra precautionary allowance for either the hoped-for death of the patient or a modification of the physician's initial opinion. (It is recognized that in accident cases involving brain damage, the forty-eight hours is critical for brain swelling.) At the termination of the imposed forty-eight-hour waiting period, if there is no modification of the physician's opinion, the will must be filed and probate started.

After the petition to probate a living will is filed—the petition can be a simple form setting up the living will as an exhibit—the court shall be required to docket the will for hearing within forty-eight hours and shall immediately issue process for service upon all necessary parties along with notice to the designated statutory parties of interest. There is ample precedence for this type of immediate court hearing; it is specified in workmen's compensation proceedings and in many matters in need of injunctive relief. At the same time, the court shall subpoena hospital records and attending physicians. The physician's appearance at the hearing shall be mandatory. If the probate is not contested, the decision of the court will be final, and the court decree shall direct the fulfillment of the patient's requests to be carried out within thirty-six hours of the court's decision; however, in the event of a contest, the constitutional right of appeal must be allowed for. Such appeal shall pass directly to the state supreme court. This particular appellate procedure exists at this time in certain types of cases and should present no problem (Tennessee C.P.R. 65:04).

The problem, however, would be a subsequent appeal to the Supreme Court of the United States. This fact must be recognized and cannot be dealt with. Until the constitutionality of a legislative act authorizing the living will has been ruled on by the Supreme Court, such an appeal would be expected. After such a ruling, a disgruntled party could force a lengthy delay by following all of the avenues of appeal. This appellate action would perhaps be discouraged by the expenses involved and by public condemnation of proceeding against the direct written wishes of the patient and hence should be only a remote problem.

Enforcement

This brings us now to a consideration of the final condition, enforcement of the court's decision to grant the right to die. The issues to be raised here will be presented because of the conflict of rights that would be initiated under any decision of a court sustaining a living will. While the decree of a court will be clear and precise in its pronouncement directing an affirmative relief action, it must also specify who is to carry it out and how. If a patient is being maintained biologically alive totally by artificial measures and if cessation of these means is not against the physician's or the hospital's moral principles, the court decree will enjoin the doctor and hospital from any further use of those measures. A similar procedure will be employed when there is self-supportive biological life; the court order will direct the administering of painless life-terminating drugs.

Any action taken in compliance with a court decree must be witnessed by all the necessary parties to the litigation, if possible. This would include all members of the family, a representative of the hospital, and the attending physician. The precise moment for complying with the court's decree *shall* be in all cases private and unannounced. A possible beneficial result of this collective witnessing might be the reduction of society's denial of death and a sharing of the emotional feelings the situation is bound to produce. Certainly a family would have the seldom realized moment of a shared communion among loved ones at death's appointed time. This alone is an often denied right.

In the situation in which a family or a physician exercises his moral rights of nonparticipation in the termination of a patient's life (and recognition of these rights must be granted by the court in its inquiry), the court's decree will direct the hospital to furnish a representative or agent to comply with the patient's request. In this day this request should present no problem, since aides, nurses, and even orderlies are used currently to turn respirators off. If the treating institution has assumed a particular moral position with reference to euthanasia (for example, Catholic hospitals, which oppose active euthanasia), this position must be explained to the court and taken into consideration by the court in reaching a final decision. An agent not employed by the hospital could be directed to carry out the court's order if necessary.

One final issue must be resolved in any court deliberation and decree sustaining a living will. It is perhaps, at this moment in medical history, the most critical issue—that of civil liability. A court order holding for the rights of a living will must at the same time absolve any and all necessary parties of any civil liability. This, of course, would stop and preclude a malpractice suit being filed against the doctors and the hospital involved, as well as a suit against the moving family members. It would also preclude any other type of tort or contractual liability theory that might evolve out of patient-physician relationship. Without this total absolution of legal responsibility and guarantee of nonliability, it is doubtful whether any physician or hospital would risk testimony of a medical determination that would satisfy the evidentiary standards. It must also be pointed out that there would be no criminal penalties because of the legislative act establishing the right to die under a living will.

It is conceded that to grant such a right of nonliability would result in a surrender of a corresponding right of an injured party to damages for malpractice; however, there must be the presumption of a waiver to this right in the contemplation and execution of a will. There is no way for a living will to work effectively without the surrender and release of this right. That is why the physician and the appointed medical panel can be expected to conclude, as far as can be determined medically, an opinion on the permanency of the patient's coma. It is the individual's reasonable contemplation of a prolonged suffering or a vegetated state that dismisses the right to recover damages when the right to die is exercised. The two rights are not compatible and cannot exist at the same time once the contemplated living will has been turned into a reality. Of course, it must be provided here that, while conscious, the patient may revoke the living will at any time and reassert the right to damages as the superior right.

Finally, there is another type of liability, which would be incurred by the family or hospital in failing to offer the living will for probate. Probating the living will would be a mandatory requirement, and any violation would subject the violator to punitive damages and personal liability for all of the prevailing and continuing medical costs. Also, a hospital should be required, upon admitting a patient for any reason, to inquire about whether there is a living will and to note the presence of a will on the medical record. If the patient does not have a will, a statutory form could be furnished at that time. Another benefit of the hospital inquiry would be that the physician, as well as the hospital, would be notified of the will, and the physician's acceptance of the case would serve as a waiver of any objections he or she might voice on moral grounds.

A concluding statement is offered to those who feel that living wills are too vague to offer any confidence in the adequacy of their safeguards. It might be pointed out that these documents could be individually tailored to mitigate some of the uncertainties about the actual intent under particular circumstances. For example, a Jehovah's Witness, opposed to blood transfusions on religious principles, could so provide in such a document. A Christian Scientist could indicate through such a document that he or she does not wish any medical treatment that might or might not terminate life. The right to these types of qualifying elements would be expressly permitted by the legislative act and detracts in no way from the procedural safeguards outlined in this chapter. (Brandt, 1977; Kaplan, 1976).

It is time to take stock of what has been discussed and offered here. In looking at the *Quinlan* case in retrospect, we can recognize the soundness of the procedural arguments that have been presented. If the court had had before it a valid living will executed by Karen, the prolonged and costly litigation would have been avoided. Because there was a reasonable doubt at the initial signing, probate of the will would have been denied. However, once the irreversibility had been established, as it was on appeal to the supreme court of New Jersey, the will would have been declared valid and a decree issued by the court directing disuse of life-prolonging equipment and thus perhaps the termination of Karen's life. As it is, Karen continues her vegetated existence in a nursing home.

Ω

Conclusion

We began our examination of suicide and euthanasia by asking several questions: What does jumping off a bridge have to do with the mercy killing of a person presumed to be dying with an irreversible disease? How can the despair and irrationality associated with suicide be linked to the compassionate concern expressed by those who would commit euthanasia to end suffering? What, if any, is the relationship between suicide and euthanasia?

The relationship between suicide and euthanasia can be seen first, we argued, in the nature of death itself. Death is not an instantaneous event but occurs in stages: respiration dies; then circulation dies some time later, to be followed by the deaths of the brain and finally the cells. Because the process of death is frequently reversible until the stage of inactivity in the brain is reached, contemporary medical definitions of death are based on brain activity—or actually the lack of it. Death is a process, one with stages or types of deaths. The reversibility of the process depends upon available technology. In a future when cloning becomes possible, the definition of death, that is, the point at which the process may be said to be irreversible, may well be the death of every cell in the body.

The stages in the process of death, although of critical importance, fail in our opinion to capture the truly human meaning of death, that is, its social nature. According to our conception of death as social, more than electrical discharges are necessary to constitute life. That is, while we may be alive by medical definitions of death if we do not have a flat EEG, if that were the total of our response, few would say we were alive in any human sense.

Death as social in our terms involves the loss of persona, of the self. For some, death occurs only when there is no possibility that an individual will ever again be able to maintain a self—to be a person to another. For others, death occurs when they no longer are able to be who they think they are—who they want to be. An accident, a stroke, a disease strikes and the person they knew themselves to be dies—leaving either a personless body or a self transformed.

To cease to be one's self, voluntarily or because of forces outside one's control, is in fact to die. Having thus already died socially, from the person we were, it is only right, proper, and dignified that our physical body should follow where our social self has already gone.

To observe the social nature of death, we examined the survivors' reactions to those who committed social suicide. Although the survivors that Weitzman studied later learned that their spouses had only feigned death, for them the death was real. They continued to grieve and to think of themselves as widows or widowers. When the insurance agents told them that their spouses were alive, they did not ask where they were, nor did they ever make any attempt to communicate with them. For the survivors, those who committed social suicide were indeed dead. The persons the survivors knew had died and they felt grief over their loss. For those who had committed social suicide, their old selves—their former personas—had died for them too.

Then we considered how cancer may rob an individual of persona, leading some to suicide. Comparing rates of suicide and psychological and psychiatric profiles, Danto concluded that for some cancer patients the loss of social function was more important than physical deterioration. Once again, in our terms Danto's cancer patients who committed suicide seemed to be saying death is social—it is the loss of persona.

Empirical reality, however, as Fletcher immediately pointed out in the third selection, cannot tell us what ought to be. To answer the questions concerning the morality of suicide and euthanasia, we must leave the world of empirical science and enter that of ethics. In Fletcher's article and in Graber's, the ethical foundations for suicide became evident. While Fletcher established his defense of suicide on situational ethics, rejecting the old absolutes of categorical rights and wrongs, Graber differentiated types of suicide, some of which had to be seen as ethical, moral, and rational. Graber's analysis also established the important point that "in judging whether a person would be better off dead, we must take into account not only the person's present and future values but also his or her personal ideals and personal integrity."

When we examine the personal circumstances in which suicide takes place, we realize that there are different types of suicide. Rather than involving social death or any right to die, some types of suicide stem from the lack of opportunity in life. The type of suicide that Wallace called murderous cannot be considered to involve the suicide's right to die because another's life is endangered. To consider as legitimate, acceptable, or justifiable any of the three types of nonjustifiable suicide is to confuse the necessarily a priori right to live with rights based on presumption of a full and satisfactory life.

In conformity with Graber's and Fletcher's arguments for analyzing the personal and individual situations within which a person acts, Wallace characterized justifiable suicide as not being done with malice or feelings of worthlessness or lack of control. In justifiable suicide the person has usually put his or her affairs in order, cared for the survivors, and said good-bye, although such messages were not always heard.

In the cases that Wallace reviewed, why did some persons wish to die? Within the conception of death pursued herein, death was sought because persona had already been lost. Thus Mr. Sullivan —feeling that he would soon lose his autonomy, his independence, his ability to care for himself and make his own decisions, especially about medical matters—chose suicide. He feared the loss of who he thought he was, who he thought he had to be.

Were Mr. Sullivan's fears justified? Twycross began his article with a quote stating that dying in pain should not be the only available alternative. Pain can be controlled. If it is not controlled, people may be driven to suicide. Such individuals cannot be thought to have chosen death. Twycross reviewed cases of his own and of others to document the effect that the control of pain can produce. Removed from death-inducing pain, those who previously may have begged to be killed may die with dignity.

Clearly it is the quality of life that is at stake once death is acknowledged to be social. Eser then examined legal statutes that have attempted and currently attempt to deal with the quality of life issue while preserving its sanctity. His historical scholarship revealed that the concerns of those both for and against sanctity or quality are well-founded. For just as the exclusive preoccupation with sanctity produces suffering for the living and the dying, for those with and those without persona, so too does exclusive pursuit of quality of life.

Whose quality is to be taken as the measure of the worthiness of life? What life is to be forced to live on, continued by machines? One answer Americans give is that they should be able to choose for themselves. A living will is an instrument by which some attempt to exercise the choice they believe they should have. But who knows of his or her end? Alive and well today, we make decisions that may significantly differ from what we will want when our time comes. These are some of the complexities of the attempt to achieve a good death that Marsh explored in our final selection. For our own protection and for others, we ought not rush into anything as final as death.

Death-related issues are indeed complex. Their complexity palls, however, in the presence of what Ernst Becker called our terror of death. And it is our terror, far more than any complexity, that interferes with our understanding. For several generations past, death-related issues were treated with denial. For years there was virtually no public and very little private discussion of death. Today previous avoidance of the unavoidable has given way to widespread discussion, debate, and even research.

Although each of the contributors has taken a position, especially the editors, it is to the public debate of the issues of suicide and euthanasia that we hope to make our greatest contribution. Not to argue, to discuss, to debate, and to deliberately consider death-related topics like suicide and euthanasia—that would be by far the greater harm. We may not be able to see, as Norman O. Brown puts it, in our old adversary, a friend – nor will our discussion necessarily lead to the embrace of a lived, compelling illusion that does not lie about life, death, and reality as Becker would have it – but discussion will certainly be preferable to silence, as light is over darkness.

Ω

Bibliography

Achté, K.A., M. Apo, and L. Happaniemi

1963 Suicide in Finland, 1954–58. *Annals Medical Society Finland* 2: 77–83.

Achté, K.A., and M.L. Vaukonen

1966 Suicider pa allmanskihus nord. *Psyktidsskr* 20:298–306.

1971 Suicides committed in general hospitals. *Psychiatria Fennica* Vol. 88, 8:221–28.

Aitken-Swan, J.

1959 Nursing the late cancer patient at home. *Practitioner* 183:64–69.

Aquinas, Thomas

1266 *Summa Theologica.* Ed. A.F. Utz. Recht und Perechtigkeit 1953:18. Heidelberg-München: Kerle.

Auer, A.

1977 Die Unverfügbarkeit des Lebens und das Recht auf eninen naturlichen Tod in A. Auer, H. Menzel, and A. Eser. *Zwischen Heilauftrag and Sterebehilfe.* Köln: Heymann.

Austrian Penal Code

S 78.

Ayres, John H., and Carol Bird

1932 *Missing men.* Garden City, N.Y.: Doubleday.

Baltrusch, H.J.

1963 Psyche, Nervensystem, neoplastischer Prozess ein altes Probem mit neuer Aktualität II Ztschr. *Psycho-Somatiche Medizin* (Oct./Dec.)9:229–45.

Bartee v. *Thompson*
67 Tennessee Reports 508.
Becker, Ernest
1973 *The denial of death.* New York: Free Press.
1977 The heroics of everyday life: a theorist of death confronts his own end. In a conversation with Sam Keen in *Readings in aging and death,* ed. Sleven H. Zarit. New York: Harper.
Behnke, John A., and Sissela Bok, eds.
1973 *The dilemmas of euthanasia.* Garden City, N.Y.: Doubleday.
Bohannon, Paul, ed.
1960 *Homicide and suicide.* Princeton: Princeton Univ. Press.
British Medical Journal
1971 Vocational training for general practice. 2:704–5.
Bonhoeffer, D.
1949 Ethik. In A. Auer, H. Menzel, and A. Eser. *Die Unverfügbarkeit des Lebens und das Recht aut einen natürlichen Tod.* München: Kaiser.
Brandt, Richard B.
1975 The morality and nationality of suicide. In *A handbook for the study of suicide,* ed. Perlin Seymour. Oxford: Oxford Univ. Press.
Brandt, Jonathan
1977 Beyond Quinlan and Saikewicz: developing standards for decisions not to treat terminally ill patients. *Boston Bar Journal* 21 (June): 5–13.
Bvertge, S.
1976 West German abortion decision: a contrast to Roe v. Wade. *The John Marshall Journal of Practice and Procedure* 9:605–42.
California Assembly
Bill 3060.
Caplow, Theodore
1973 Preface. In Wallace, 1973.
Carolina
1532 Arts. 106; 109, 111, 116; 119, 124–27; 130; 133; 135; 162; 172; 192.
Churchill, Allen
1960 *They never came back.* Garden City, New York: Doubleday.
Conrad, Joseph
1910 *The secret sharer.* New York: Harper.
Craig, T.J., and M.D. Abelhoff
1974 Psychiatric symptomology among hospitalized cancer patients. *American Journal of Psychiatry* 131:1223–27.
Crichton, Robert
1959 *The great imposter.* New York: Random House.
Danto, B.L.
1973 The cancer patient and suicide. In *Agents for the Terminally*

Ill and Bereaved, ed. I. Goldberg, S. Malitz, R.A.H. Kutscher, pp. 36–41. New York: Columbia Univ. Press.

Dollard, J.
1939 *Frustration and aggression.* New Haven: Yale Univ. Press.

Dorpat, T.L., W.F. Anderson, and H.S. Ripley
1968 The relationship of physical illness to suicide. In *Suicide behaviors: diagnosis and management by 48 authors*, ed. H.L.P. Resnik, pp. 209–19. Boston: Little, Brown.

Douglas, Jack D.
1967 *The social meanings of suicide.* Princeton: Princeton Univ. Press.

Downing, A.B., ed.
1969 *Euthanasia and the right to death: the case for voluntary euthanasia.* London: Peter Owen.

Dubovsky, S.L.
1978 Averting suicide in terminally ill patients. *Psychosomatics* 19 (Feb.):113–15.

Durkheim, Emile
1951 *Suicide*, trans. John A. Spaulding and George Simpson. New York: Free Press.

Eckhardt, A. Roy
1973 Death in the Judaic and Christian traditions. In *Death in American experience*, ed. Arien Mack. New York: Schocken.

Ellison, Ralph
1952 *Invisible Man.* New York: New American Library.

Eser, A.
1976a Justification and excuse. *American Journal of Comparative Law* 24:618–28.
1976b *Suizid und Euthanasie als human-und sozialwissenschaftliches Problem.* Stuggart: Enke.
1977a Zwischen "Heiligkeit" und "Qualität" des Lebens. Zu Wandlungen im strafrechtlichen Lebensschutz. In *Tradition und Fortschritt im Recht. Festschrift zum 500 jährigen Bestehen der Tübinger Juristenfakultät.* Tübingen: Mohr/Siebeck.
1977b In A. Auer, H. Menzel, and A. Eser. *Zwischen Heilauftrag und Sterbehilfe.* Köln: Heyman.
1980 In A. Schönke and H. Schröder, eds. *Kommentar zum Strafgesetzbuch.* 20th ed. S, 212 note 6 S. 218, 218a.

Farberow, Norman L., and Edwin S. Shneidman
1961 *The cry for help.* New York: McGraw-Hill.

Farberow, N., S. Ganzler, F. Cutler, and D. Reynolds
1971 An eight-year survey of hospital suicides. *Life Threatening Behavior* 1 (Fall):184–202.

Farberow, N.L., J.W. McKelligott, S. Cohen and A. Darbonne
1966 Suicide among patients with cardiorespiratory illnesses. *Jour-*

nal of American Medical Association 195 (Feb. 7):422–28.
Farberow, N.L., E.S. Shneidman and C.V. Leonard
1963 Suicide among general medical and surgical hospital patients with malignant neoplasm. *Medical Bulletin* 9 (Feb.) 1008–1028. Veterans Administration, Department of Medicine and Surgery.
Feifel, Herman
1977 *New meanings of death.* New York: McGraw-Hill.
Ferri, Enrico
1925 *L'omicidio-Suicidio.* Torino: Bocca.
Festus
1899 As cited by Mommsen, 1899.
Feuerbach, J.P.A.
1813 *Anmerkungen zum Strafgesetzbuch für das Königreich Bayern,* vol. II. München.
1826 *Lehrbuch des Gemeinen in Deutschland gültigen peinlichen Rechts.* 9th ed. Giessen: Heyer.
Freud, Sigmund
1933 *Collected papers.* London: Highgate.
Geilen, G.
1974 Suizid und Mitverantwortung. *Juristenzeitung* 29:145.
German Basic Law
Art. 102.
German Penal Code
S 211; S 220a, section 1, no. 1, in combination with section 2; S 281a, section 2, no. 3; S 216.
Gibbs, Jack P. and Walter T. Martin
1964 *Status, integration and suicide: a sociological study.* Eugene: Univ. of Oregon Press.
Glaser, B., and Anslem Strauss
1965 *Awareness of dying.* Chicago: Aldine.
1968 *Time for dying.* Chicago: Aldine.
1971 *Status passage.* Chicago: Aldine.
Goffman, Erving
1959 *The presentation of self in everyday life.* New York: Doubleday.
1961 *Asylums.* Garden City, N.Y.: Anchor.
Gold, Martin
1958 *Homicide and suicide.* Boston: Allyn and Bacon.
Harvard Medical School, Ad Hoc Committee to Examine the Definition of Brain Death
1968 A definition of irreversible coma. *Journal of American Medical Association* 205 (Aug. 5):337–40.
Henry, Andrew A., and James F. Short
1954 *Suicide and homicide.* Glencoe: Free Press.

Henslin, James A.
1977 Guilt and guilt neutralization: response and adjustment to suicide. In *Deviance and respectability,* ed. Jack Douglas. New York: Basic Books.
Hindeman, William P., Jr.
1965 The presumption against suicide in disappearance cases. *Insurance Law Journal* 514 (Nov.):645–50.
Hinschius, P.
1888 *System des katholischen Kirchenrechts* 4:31–47.
1893 *System des katholischen Kirchenrechts* 5:798.
Hull v. *Evans*
59 Tennessee Appeals Reports 193
Jalet, Frances T.F.
1968 Mysterious disappearance: the presumption of death and the administration of the estates of missing persons or absentees. *Iowa Law Review* 54 (Oct.):177–252.
Jourard, Signey M.
1969 The invitation to die. In *On the nature of suicide,* ed. Edwin S. Schneidman. San Francisco: Jossey-Bass.
Kalish, Robert
1968 Life and death: dividing the invisible. *Social Science and Medicine* 2:249–50.
Kansas Statutes Annotated
Section 77–202.
Kaplan, Ronald
1976 Euthanasia legislation: a survey and a model act. *American Journal of Law and Medicine* 2 (Summer):41–99.
Kirkpatrick v. *Kirkpatrick*
61 Tennessee Reports 342.
Kobler, A.L., and Ezra Stotland
1964 *The end of hope.* New York: Free Press.
Kohl, Marvin
1974 *The morality of killing.* New York: Humanities Press.
Lenckner, Th.
1980 In A. Schönke and H. Schröder, eds. *Kommentar zum Strafgesetzbuch.* 20th ed., S 34, note 23 ss.
Lindeman, Eric
1944 Symptomology and management of acute grief. *American Journal of Psychiatry* 101:141–48.
Litin, E.M.
1960 What shall we tell the cancer patient? A psychiatrist's view. *Proceedings Mayo Clinic* 35:247–50.
Lofland, Lyn H.
1976 *Toward a sociology of death and dying.* Beverly Hills, Calif.: Sage.

1978 *The craft of dying.* Beverly Hills, Calif.: Sage.

Margolis, Joseph
1975 *Negativities: the limit of life.* Columbus, Ohio: Merrill.

Maris, Ronald
1969 *Social forces in urban suicide.* Homewood, Ill.: Dorsey.

Marks, Alan
1977 Religious orthodoxy: religious participation and moral evaluation of suicide. Paper presented to the Southern Sociological Society, Atlanta.

Marks, R.M., and E.J. Sachar
1973 Undertreatment of medical inpatients with narcotic analgesics. *Annals of Internal Medicine* 78:173–81.

Marshall, V.
1975 Impending death in a retirement village. *American Journal of Sociology* 80:1124–44.

Menninger, Karl A.
1938 *Man against himself.* New York: Harcourt.

Millard, C.K.
1931 *Euthanasia.* London: C.W. Daniel.

Mommsen, Thomas
1899 *Römisches Staatsrecht.* S 612, 616, 617. Leipzig: Verlag Duncker and Humblot.

Montell, William
1975 *Ghosts along the Cumberland: deathlore in the Kentucky foothills.* Knoxville: Univ. of Tennessee Press.

Mueller, G.O.W.
1958 On common law men's rea. *Minnesota Law Review* 42:88–98.

Nelson, F.L., and N.L. Farberow
1976 Indirect suicide in the elderly, chronically ill patient. *Suicide Research: Psychiatria Fennica Supplementum 8:125–39.*

New German Penal Code
1976 S 218A.

Northern, State v.
563 S.W. 2d 197.

Porterfield, Austin L.
1959 Indices of suicide and homicide by states and cities. *American Sociological Review* 14:4.
1960 Traffic fatalities, suicide, and homicide. *American Sociological Review* 25:2.

Quetelet, Adolphe
1835 *Sur l'homme le developpement de ses facultés ou essai de physique sociale.* Paris: Bachelier.

Quinlan
In re: Karen, No. C-201-75, Superior Court, New Jersey.

Quinney, Richard
1965 Suicide, homicide, and economic development. *Social Forces* 43:3.

Radburch, G., and A. Kaufmann
1975 Peinliche Gerichtsordnung Kaiser Karls V. von 1532. [German title of the Carolina]. Stuttgart: Reclam Universal Bibliothek Nr. 2990/90a.

Rakoff, Vivian M.
1973 Psychiatric aspects of death in America. In *Death in American experience,* ed. Arien Mack. New York: Schocken.

Reiser, M.
1966 Retrospects and prospects. *New York Academy of Sciences* 124:1044.

Roe v. *Wade*
1973 410 U.S.: 113, 158, 163.

Rosshirt, K.F.
1839 *Geschichte und System des deutschen Strafrechts.* Stuttgart: Metzler.

Russell, O. Ruth
1975 *Freedom to die: moral and legal aspects of euthanasia.* New York: Dell.

Sainsbury, P.
1955 *Suicide in London: an ecological study.* London: Chapman and Hall; rpt. New York: Basic Books, 1956.

Sanders, Joseph
1977 Euthanasia: none dare call it murder. In *Death and society,* ed. James P. Carse and Arlene Dallery. New York: Harcourt.

Saunders, C.
1973 A death in the family: a professional view. *British Medical Journal* 1:30–31.

Schmidt, E.
1965 *Einführung in die Geschichte der deutschen Strafrechtspflege.* 3d ed. Göttingen: Vandenhoeck & Ruprecht.

Schönke, A.
1942 *Strafgesetzbuch für das Deutsche Reich.* S 218, note V. 2. München: Beck.

Schorer, C.E.
1961 The fantastic psychopathology of cancer patients, *Michigan Medicine* (June):535–36.

Schowing, J.
1974 Teratologie. *Image Roche* 63:2 (Basel: Hoffman La Roche).

Shneidman, Edwin S., ed.
1967 *Essays in self-destruction.* New York: Aronson.
1969 *On the nature of suicide.* San Francisco: Jossey-Bass.

1973 *Deaths of man.* New York: Times Books; rpt. Penguin, 1974.
Shneidman, Edwin S., and Norman L. Farberow
1957 *Clues to suicide.* New York: McGraw-Hill.
Silving, Helen
1954 Euthanasia: a study in comparative law. *University of Pennsylvania Law Review* 3:408–427.
1957 Suicide and law. In Shneidman and Farberow, 1957.
Simson, G.
1976 *Die Suizidtat.* 42 ss.
Simson, G., and F. Geerdo
1969 *Straftaten gegen die Person und Sittlichkeitsdelikte in rechtsvergleichender Sicht.* München: Beck.
Spangenberg, S.
1818 Über das Verbrechen der Abreibung der Leibesfrucht. *Archiv des Criminalrechts* 2:1–53, 173–93.
Stannard, David E.
1973 Death and dying in Puritan New England. *American Historical Review* (Dec.):1305–30.
State v. *Northern*
563 S.W. 2d 197.
Stenback, A.
1972 Suicide and bodily integrity. *Psychiatria Fennica* 289–90.
Stewart, I.
1957 Organic disease and suicide. *Lancet* 1:1355.
1960 Suicide: the influence of organic disease. *Lancet* 2:919.
Stricklin v. *State*
497 S.W. 2d 755.
Sudnow, David
1967 *Passing on: the social organization of dying.* Englewood Cliffs, N.J.: Prentice-Hall.
Supreme Court of Tennessee
Civil Procedure, Rule 17:02.
Civil Procedure, Rule 22:01.
Civil Procedure, Rule 65:04.
Swiss Penal Code
Art. 115.
Tennessee Code Annotated
Section 53–549.
Section 34–1008.
Section 32–101–108.
Section 50–1018–25.
C.P.R. (Civil Procedure Rule) 22:01; 65:04.
Turnbull, F.
1954 Intractable pain. *Proceedings of the Royal Society of Medicine* 47:155–56.

Twycross, R.G.
1974 Clinical experience with diamorphine in advanced malignant disease. *International Journal of Clinical Pharmacology, Therapy and Toxicology* 9:184–98.
U.S., Department of Health, Education and Welfare
1967 *Suicide in the United States 1950–1964.* National Center for Health Statistics, Washington, D.C. Series 20, no. 5 (Aug.): 1–11.
Veatch, Robert M.
1977 Death and dying: the legislative options. *The Hastings Center Report* 7 (Oct.):5.
Verkko, Veli
1951 *Homicides and suicides in Finland.* Kobenhavn, private.
Vernon, G.
1970 *Sociology of death: an analysis of death-related behavior.* New York: Ronald.
Von Hentig, Hans
1940 Remarks on the interaction of perpetrator and victim. *Journal of Criminal Law and Criminology* 31:3.
Wächter, G.C.
1826 *Lehrbuch des romischteutschen Stratfrechts* 12:173–79.
1829 Revision der Lehre von dem Selbstmorde, nach dem positiven und gemeinen Deutschen Rechte und den neuen Gesetzgebungen. *Archiv des Criminalrechts* 10:646.
Wallace, Samuel E., and Jose M. Canals
1962 Socio-legal aspects of a study of acts of violence. *American University Law Review* 11:2.
Wallace, Samuel E.
1973 *After Suicide.* New York: Wiley-Interscience.
Weisman, A.D.
1974 *The realization of death.* New York: Aronson.
Wertenbaker, Lael
1957 *Death of a man.* Random House.
Williams, Glanville L.
1957 *The sanctity of life and the criminal law.* New York: Knopf.

Ω

Notes on the Contributors

Bruce L. Danto, M.D., is Director, Suicide Prevention and Drug Information Center, Detroit Psychiatric Institute.

Albin Eser, M.C.J., is Professor of Criminal and Comparative Law at the University of Tübingen, West Germany; Judge at the Upper State Court at Stuttgart; and Commentator of the German Penal Code.

Joseph Fletcher, Ph.D., is Visiting Scholar in Biomedical Ethics, School of Medicine, University of Virginia; Robert Treat Paine Professor Emeritus of Social Ethics, Episcopal Divinity School, Cambridge, Massachusetts; and President Emeritus of the Society for the Right To Die.

Glenn C. Graber, Ph.D., is Associate Professor in the Department of Philosophy, University of Tennessee, Knoxville; Chair of the Committee on Graduate Study in Medical Ethics; and Associate Editor of *The Journal of Religious Ethics.*

Frank H. Marsh, Ph.D. and D.J., is Associate Professor in the Department of Philosophy, Old Dominion University, with specialization in bioethics and philosophy of law.

Robert G. Twycross, D.M., M.C.R.P., is Consultant Physician, in charge of Sir Michael Sobell House, The Churchill Hospital, Headington, Oxford, England.

Samuel E. Wallace, Ph.D., is Professor of Sociology; and Chair of the Urban Studies Program, University of Tennessee, Knoxville.

Lenore J. Weitzman, Ph.D., is with the Divorce Law Research Project, Center for the Study of Law and Society, University of California, Berkeley.

Ω

Index